ADVANCE PR

It's one thing to clear the clutter out of your house; it's another to know what the heck to do with the stuff you're keeping. Thank heaven we have Donna Smallin to solve that problem for us. And she does it brilliantly!

Gail Blanke, Author of *Throw Out Fifty Things: Clear the Clutter, Find Your Life*

This book should be a key reference on any homeowner's shelf. I love the creative ideas for inexpensive solutions and the tips and quotes throughout that motivate and inspire.

Lorie Marrero, CPO, Creator of the Clutter Diet

Donna Smallin has advanced her cause mightily with this must-have handbook of practical (and nifty) ideas and strategies for storing those "surviving" household possessions that are worth keeping!

Ciji Ware, author of *Rightsizing Your Life: Simplifying Your Surroundings While Keeping What Matters Most*

This book covers everything! From Addresses to X-Rays, Donna Smallin tells you where to store and how to organize practically everything in your life!

Monica Ricci, author of *Organizing Your Office in No Time* and Office Depot spokesperson

The *One-Minute Organizer*
A to Z Storage Solutions

The One-Minute Organizer
A to Z Storage Solutions

DONNA SMALLIN

Storey Publishing

The mission of Storey Publishing is to serve our customers by publishing practical information that encourages personal independence in harmony with the environment.

Edited by Lisa Hiley and Deborah Balmuth
Art direction and book design by Mary Winkelman Velgos
Text production by Jennifer Jepson Smith

Illustrations by © Juliette Borda
Author photo by Peter LaMastro/Sublime Management

Indexed by Nancy D. Wood

Printed in the United States by Dickinson Press
10 9 8 7 6 5 4 3 2 1

Library of Congress Cataloging-in-Publication Data
Smallin, Donna, 1960–
The one-minute organizer A to Z storage solutions / Donna Smallin.
p. cm.
Includes index.
ISBN 978-1-60342-084-6 (paper : alk. paper)
1. Storage in the home. 2. House cleaning. 3. Orderliness.
I. Title. II. Title: 1-minute organizer A to Z storage solutions.
TX309.S627 2009
648'.8—dc22

2008040090

To my husband, Mike Kuper,
my favorite person to spend time with:
Your love and support are too wonderful for words.

ACKNOWLEDGMENTS

I give thanks to family members, friends, and colleagues for their contributions: my assistant, Julie Moran; organizing coach, Marlo Nikkila; my sister-in-law, Cori Peel; my piano teacher, Debbie Saifi; all my friends at Storey Publishing; and to my parents, Clarence and Lorraine Connor, who taught me most of what I know about organizing — without me even realizing it.

Thanks, also, to fellow members of the National Association of Professional Organizers for teaching me the rest of what I've learned.

I am especially grateful to my readers. Your questions, challenges, and stories inspire and support my mission to help others create more time for the people and things they love.

Contents

Storage Solutions

Out of the Box Organizers

PREFACE

ARE YOU TIRED OF SEARCHING for things you know are "around here somewhere"? Have you had it with what you not-so-fondly refer to as "this mess"? Do you think maybe you need a bigger home to store all your stuff? Maybe you're right. Or maybe you just need to free up some space and create a place for everything so you can put everything in its place.

In this big little book of storage solutions, you'll find some of my favorite tips and ideas for storing everything from art supplies, batteries, and clothing to wine, X-rays, and yoga equipment. I've also included space-saving and economical solutions as well as ready-made and do-it-yourself solutions.

I wrote this book to answer the question I hear most often: What do I do with this? It's an A-to-Z guide so you can find quick answers to your specific questions about how to organize items for everyday, seasonal, and long-term storage. Note that this book is less about uncluttering and organizing (though I do encourage both!) and more about how to properly store things and make the best use of storage space.

While there are some hard-and-fast storage rules (such as don't store leather or fur in plastic), you may be surprised to discover that there's no one *right* way to store most stuff. The right solution is the one that works for you. That's why I've provided a number of different options . . . so you can choose the solution that feels right.

If you need help getting started, choose one storage solution from this book and try it. Start today with "A." My hope is that once you find a place for everything, you'll be able to find everything you want, when you want it. Ahhh . . . the simplicity of it.

When people ask me if I've always been organized, I have to say yes.

I was one of those kids who didn't need to be told to make her bed or put away her toys. I just did it.

I remember a time when I was about 11 years old. I went over to my friend Julie's house to play. I had never been in her room before, and let's just say that it didn't look anything like my room. There were dolls and toys and clothes and stuff strewn all over the place. I couldn't walk in the room without stepping on something. There was no way I could play in that room without straightening it up first!

I was having fun gathering and putting Barbie's clothes and shoes into her case. But after about 15 minutes, Julie said to me, "You're boring."

Is that what you think about organizing and storing your stuff? That it's boring? I might agree with you except for one thing: I've learned that the rewards are well worth the effort. As you go through the process of getting all your stuff in order, you will create more time, space, and energy for the things that really matter, which, of course, are not things at all.

Introduction

Before you read any further, I want you to think about something. What do you believe is the biggest obstacle you face when it comes to organizing your stuff? Is it . . .

Lack of space? According to a survey by the National Soap & Detergent Association, 80 percent of clutter in most homes is the result of disorganization, not lack of space.

Lack of time? In a 2008 poll conducted on behalf of the National Association of Professional Organizers (NAPO), 19 percent of women and 11 percent of men anticipate they'd save more than an hour each day if they were more organized, for a total of 15 days annually.

Lack of money? There's no need to run out and spend money on fancy organizing products. Look around. See what you have that might do the trick — at least temporarily. That way, you'll have a better idea of what you need should you decide to upgrade later. For examples of common items that can be transformed into storage solutions, look for the "Out of the Box Organizers" highlighted throughout this book.

Lack of know-how? All of the suggestions in this book are based on the following seven principles of good storage. Let this quick lesson be your guide as you figure out what to do with your stuff.

1 Unclutter first.

The average U.S. home has doubled in size in the last 60 years and still we struggle to find a place for everything. Hmmm . . . could it be we have too much stuff? My motto is "If you don't love it or use it, lose it."

Why bother storing things you don't use? Eliminate all the unnecessary "necessities." Get rid of duplicates. Do you really need three vegetable peelers? If you're keeping something "just in case," ask yourself: Could I get this again pretty easily and inexpensively if I need it again someday? If the answer is yes, let it go.

And let's face it. Everything has a life span. Chuck anything that is unusable or unfixable. Are you storing things for grown children? You may be saving things they don't even want! Question everything.

2 Pick a space, but not just any space.

Where you store items depends on a variety of factors. First, gather everything that needs to be stored in one place so you can see how much storage space you need. Allow room for future expansion as with a music, video, or other type of collection. Store frequently used things where you use them; you'll be more likely to put them away when you're done.

Take temperature and humidity into account when considering storage locations. Fur, leather, and other natural fabrics, as well as candles, paper, paint, and many other items, have special storage requirements. Keep in mind that basements tend to be humid, which creates a breeding ground for mold and mildew. Attics and garages, on the other hand, may be too hot and dry for storing certain items.

Most important, think about safety. Always store household cleaners, prescriptions, matches, guns, knives, insecticides, paint, gasoline, and other hazardous household materials out of children's reach, preferably in locked cabinets. Store heavy items on the floor or on lower shelves. And be sure to secure personal and financial information in a lockable filing cabinet to help deter identity theft.

3 Store like with like.

It's a lot easier to know what you have — or don't have — when you store like items together. In a pantry or food cabinets, for example, organize and store items by type of food such as cereals, pastas, and rices; canned vegetables and fruits; snack foods; and so on. In closets, you might organize by type of clothing such as short-sleeved shirts, pants, and skirts.

Consider creating zones by activity. When you set up a hanging folder to store your tax records throughout the year, you are creating a zone. In the kitchen, you might create a baking zone with cookie sheets, electric mixer, and mixing bowls in one cabinet and rolling pins, measuring cups, and other baking utensils in a nearby drawer. In the garage, set up zones for storing tools and supplies for common activities such as gardening, automotive care, and sports; include a zone for general storage.

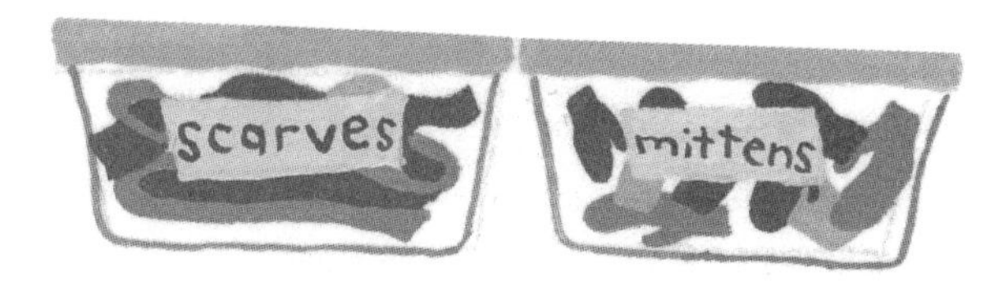

4 Consider accessibility.

Think about how you use an item and how often you use it. Store frequently used items where they are most convenient. In the kitchen, for example, you might keep your coffeemaker on the counter because you use it every day, but store the food processor in a nearby cabinet if you use it once a week or less often.

Store things you rarely use in less prime locations such as the upper shelf of a closet, back of a cabinet, or some other out-of-the way place in the basement, attic, or garage. This includes seasonal items such as clothing and holiday decorations, occasionally used items such as punch bowls and large roasting pans, and tax returns and other paper records that require long-term storage.

Easy accessibility makes a garage or shed ideal for storing frequently used outdoor items such as lawn and garden equipment and bicycles. Because the attic is typically the least accessible storage place, limit attic storage to things you need only occasionally.

5 Find or create hidden storage.

To find a place for everything, make use of vertical wall space and other hidden storage spaces. In your office or kitchen, you can hang multitiered organizers for sorting mail and storing restaurant take-out menus or magazines. Think about using the backs of doors in your closets, pantry, and utility room as storage spaces. A shoe rack hung over the back of a door, for example, takes up less space than a standing shoe rack and frees up floor space. Create a storage space or a work space in a corner of a bedroom or den with a divider screen or bookshelf.

Make use of hidden storage space under a bed, behind a sofa or door, and on top of kitchen or garage cabinets. Think about what you might be able to hang from the ceiling. Shop for furniture with built-in storage space — a lidded ottoman or bench, an entertainment center with media storage, a coffee table with drawers to store remote controls, an office armoire for your computer with storage spaces and doors to hide office supplies.

6 Maximize existing storage space.

Eliminate wasted space in cabinets. See it? Right there at the top? You can double, even triple, cabinet storage space by raising or lowering shelves.

If shelves are not adjustable, maximize storage space with freestanding shelves, under-shelf hanging baskets, stepped shelves, and double-decker turntables in a variety of sizes. In closets and on garage or basement shelves, use same-size storage boxes that stack easily to make best use of vertical space.

7 Make it easy to maintain.

There are five simple things you can do to help ensure that your storage solutions work well. First, label everything. Make labels big and bold for easy readability. Store boxes and bins with labels facing out. Label shelves, too, so that no one can use the excuse "I didn't know where to put it."

Second, don't just toss things into storage. You can fit a lot more stuff into any space when you take the time to arrange it so that it fits like pieces of a puzzle. Put things back where they belong and you won't have to spend hours or days reorganizing your storage at a future date.

Third, periodically reevaluate your storage spaces. Do you still need everything? Regular purging will help keep storage spaces organized.

Fourth, before making any purchases, ask yourself these questions: Do I love this? Do I really need it? Where will I store it? How often will I use it? Do I already have something similar? Then, keep clutter at bay with this simple rule: As you acquire new items, discard older items.

And fifth, know that when it seems like it's time to add more storage space, it's probably time to eliminate some stuff.

A to Z

#1
address

ADDRESSES

Most address books share the same challenge: people move. You can write address changes in pencil and erase as needed, use correction fluid to make changes, or live with the mess of cross-outs. Here are some better solutions:

- **A Rolodex file or address book** with replaceable cards
- **Address books** with peel-away labels
- **A lifetime address book** with laminated pages so you can wipe off outdated entries and rewrite current information
- **A computerized system** using Microsoft Outlook, Excel, Access, or other contact management software

Any of these options make it easy to update addresses. With contact management software, you can also quickly search for individual contacts, and even merge selected names and addresses to labels, letters, and envelopes. An additional benefit of using an electronic address book is that your contacts can be synchronized with a portable electronic device such as a Palm Pilot or Blackberry, which then enables you to have all that contact information at your fingertips

ONE-MINUTE SOLUTION

Proper lighting in a closet, basement, or attic can transform good storage into great storage. Use the highest wattage allowed in your lighting fixtures. If you need additional lighting, look for clip-on lamps designed to illuminate work areas or adhesive battery-powered lights.

wherever you go. Just be sure to back up your contact manager periodically.

(see also Storage Solution, page 196)

ADOPTION PAPERS

Store in a bank safe-deposit box. Give a copy to your executor.

(see also Storage Solution, page 32)

AIRLINE TICKETS *(see Tickets)*

ARTS AND CRAFTS SUPPLIES

If possible, keep arts and crafts supplies near where they are used. A rolling cart with drawers can be tucked away under a table or desk or stored in a nearby closet or pantry. Organize drawers by materials or type of craft. Within drawers, label and use large ziplock bags to sort and store items such as brushes, crayons, markers, and paint containers.

For small items such as buttons, beads, sequins, glitter, use a plastic, handled toolbox with removable dividers or a small hardware bin with multiple compartments and a snap-shut lid to keep items securely in place. Store the portable bin on top of the cart when not in use.

(see also Storage Solutions, pages 40, 153)

Filing cabinets

Every household needs at least one filing drawer; most could use a two- or three-drawer filing cabinet. If you operate a home business, store personal and business papers in separate filing cabinets or drawers. Consider designating drawers for student family members for storing graded homework and tests, artwork, report cards and other school papers.

You might also be able to use one drawer for storing office supplies. Use shoe boxes, food-storage containers, or ziplock bags to organize the contents. Or use an extra drawer to store gifts or greeting cards, filed by category or date to send. My dream kitchen has built-in drawers for filing recipes, product manuals and warranties, take-out menus, and other household papers. A rolling filing cart may have to suffice if built-in storage is not an option. *(see also Office/School Supplies; Paper; Storage Solutions, pages 196, 267)*

baskets

- Use to store craft supplies; makes it easy to take knitting or sewing projects to different rooms in the house.
- Keep a large one in the living room or family room to hold toys (for kids and pets) or slippers and a throw for chilly evenings. A small one can hold a collection of remote controls and a TV guide.
- Set up baskets for incoming and outgoing mail. Use one with compartments to hold envelopes, stamps, address labels, and other supplies.
- A lidded basket in a closet-less bathroom can hold towels and a stash of extra toilet paper.
- A collection of pretty baskets on a desk or dresser can hold a variety of office supplies, toiletries, jewelry — all sort of items!
- Use a deep, narrow basket to gather current magazines and catalogs in one handy place for reading.
- A basket with sections is a good place to gather pet medications, grooming supplies, and toys in one spot.
- A tiered hanging basket can be used to organize and store hair accessories in a bathroom or bedroom closet.

ARTWORK, CHILDREN'S

At the beginning of each school year, provide each child with a container to store artwork. You can buy special products designed for this purpose or look for economical art storage boxes, portfolios, or cases wherever art or office supplies are sold. A clean pizza box would also serve the purpose.

Label the container with the child's name and age or grade and store in a place that is easily accessible by your child, such as in a bedroom closet, under a bed, or in a drawer in the family room. Allow the size of the container to dictate when it's time to weed out the collection and retain your favorites.

Alternatively, "store" current artwork by hanging it in the child's room, in the laundry or mudroom, or behind kitchen cabinet doors. Then, as you replace older art with newer art, store your favorite pieces in the child's portfolio.

ONE-MINUTE SOLUTION

Rather than storing every piece of children's artwork, save a photograph of it. Tape the artwork to a wall and have your child pose with it. Then put the photograph in a scrapbook along with smaller items of artwork such as handmade cards. Create separate albums for each child.

AUTOMOTIVE SUPPLIES

Designate an automotive storage zone in the garage, mudroom, or basement. Store cleaning supplies, such as soap, wax, sponges, and drying and polishing cloths, in a bucket that can double as your carwash bucket. Store oil and other fluids, plus spare windshield wipers and other items, on a shelf with the bucket of cleaning supplies.

AWARDS *(see Trophies and Awards)*

B

BACKPACKS, SCHOOL

Without a home of their own, backpacks have a tendency to end up on the floor in front of the door or at the bottom of the stairs or on the kitchen table or counter. One of the simplest, most inexpensive ways to get kids to "store" their backpacks is to install hooks at their height — in a hall closet (use the back of the door if you can), entryway, or their bedrooms. A sturdy coat rack can also be used to hang backpacks as well as coats.

Stackable crates, cubbies, and shelves with bins are equally good options if you have room in a closet or entryway. The trick is training kids to put their backpacks where they belong.

BAGS, GROCERY (PAPER, PLASTIC, CLOTH)

There's no need to save every plastic or paper bag. Decide how many is enough and then return extras to the supermarket for recycling. If you save plastic bags, limit the number by storing them in a small container such as a gallon plastic jug with a hole cut in the front or an empty tissue box.

Store them on a shelf in the pantry or laundry room or wherever you most often need them, such

(continued)

Don't just put things down. **Put them away.** Even when you're in a hurry, remind yourself that it takes just a moment or two right now to hang up your coat or to file that receipt. Then do it.

Bags, Grocery (Paper, Plastic, Cloth) *(continued)*
as near the cat's litter box or with your dog's leash. Or store a few in each bathroom to use as liners for small wastebaskets.

You might even stash a few in your car; stuff them into an empty toilet tissue roll and toss the roll in the glove box. Or hang plastic bags along with a few flattened paper bags in a single bag that you can hang from a hook in a convenient place. Better yet, use sturdy canvas or string bags instead of paper or plastic and store them in your car, where you'll always have them when you need them.

BANK STATEMENTS

There are several reasons why you may want to store bank statements, the most common of which is documentation for tax-deductible business expenses (though original receipts are preferred). Bank statements may also come in handy if you're trying to track down a forgotten transaction or clarify a question in your personal or business finances. And if you apply for a mortgage or home loan, you may need to provide two or three recent bank statements as part of the application process.

It is best to do things systematically, since we are only human, and disorder is our worst enemy.

HESIOD

B

Many banks offer the option to deliver electronic statements, which you can store on your computer. Store them in folders by year.

If you choose to file paper statements, set up a hanging file folder for Bank Accounts and then create separate interior folders for each account. File statements in reverse chronological order (most current in front). You should be aware that if you withdraw money from one account and deposit it into another account, and IRS records show only the deposit, the amount deposited might be assumed to be taxable income unless proven otherwise. While you may be able to obtain a copy of those statements from your bank, it's a good idea to store all bank statements with your tax documents each year.
(see also Tax Records)

BASEBALL CARDS AND OTHER COLLECTIBLE SPORTS CARDS

The first order of business is to protect your investment. Never expose cards to direct sunlight. Store in a cool, dry place. The ideal storage temperature is between 64 and 72°F (18–22°C) with 45–55 percent humidity. High humidity can warp cards and result

ONE-MINUTE SOLUTION

If you do nothing else, store all collectible cards in a dark (not clear) plastic container with a tightly fitting lid to limit exposure to light and humidity.

in mold. Note that a dehumidifier may emit ozone, which can damage cards.

While some collectors store cards in special protector sheets that hold nine cards per page and place them in three-ring binders, most collectors put cards into individual protective sleeves, known as penny sleeves. Though they are very inexpensive, these thin plastic pouches go a long way toward preventing wear and tear; some even have UV inhibitors.

More valuable cards should be stored in what's known as a toploader, a rigid plastic cover that prevents bending and creasing. Very valuable cards are best stored in a screw-down case of hard plastic. All of these storage supplies are widely available at hobby shops.

To organize a large collection of cards, sort them (with or without sleeves) into corrugated cardboard boxes using labeled sticky notes as temporary dividers. Organize alphabetically by player, by year, or however makes sense to you. A valuable collection should be stored in a fireproof safe or bank safe-deposit box. You can also organize your collection using special card collection software or by creating a spreadsheet.

BASKETS

The cleverest way to store baskets is to use them to hold a variety of items including loose change and other pocket items, mail, shoes, kitchen or bathroom items, toys, and knitting projects. Handled baskets are useful for carting loads up and down stairs and for quick pick-up of a living area.

If you prefer not to use them, display the prettiest ones on a shelf or on top of kitchen cabinets. Baskets you use often for serving breads and chips can be stored in kitchen cabinets along with serving dishes or on top of the refrigerator for easy access.

Basement storage

Unless your basement is humidity-controlled, don't store anything directly on the floor; place all storage boxes on shelves or pallets. If flooding is a possibility, store everything in watertight plastic tubs instead of cardboard boxes.

Avoid storing newspapers and magazines in the basement, attic, or garage, as paper items will attract spiders.

Store pet food and birdseed in tightly lidded containers to protect the contents from rodents.

(see also Storage Solutions, pages 153, 175)

BATH SUPPLIES

Why not keep a basket of your favorite bath salts, eye and neck pillows, candles, and other "pamper-me" items in a basket by the tub for easy access after a stressful day?

(see also Toiletries)

BATTERIES

Store alkaline batteries in a cool, dry place. The average shelf life of alkaline batteries at room temperature is five to seven years. Freezing can prolong the charge of NiDc and NiMh batteries for up to a month. Chilled batteries need to be warmed to room temperature before using. Manufacturers do not recommend refrigerating or freezing alkaline batteries.

(see also Storage Solution, page 267)

laundry baskets

- Put a small one in the trunk of your car to hold maintenance items (windshield fluid, oil, dry gas, and rags).
- Keep summer shoes and flip flops in a basket in the mudroom or entryway. At the end of the season, the whole basket goes into storage.
- In the winter, use one to hold wet or muddy boots and save yourself some floor cleanup.
- Use them in the basement or garage to store sports equipment: one for each sport to hold helmets, skates, balls, protective padding, and so on.
- A large laundry basket can hold all your recyclables, or use several smaller ones to sort out paper, plastic, and metal.
- Keep one handy for when you're having company and you want to do a quick cleanup.

B

BEACH AND POOL GEAR

Do you load beach chairs, blankets, towels, flotation devices, and other gear into your trunk before every outing to the beach or community pool? Consider stowing those items permanently in the trunk during the swim season. It will save the time and effort of loading and reloading, plus save space in the garage or wherever you're storing these things now. If you need the trunk space temporarily for something else, take them out.

If you have a home pool, keep clean pool towels and toys in a lidded outdoor storage box or bench. Toys, flotation wings, and beach balls can be collected in a laundry basket or large plastic-mesh tote and left in the pool area or stored by the door nearest the pool. Keep a laundry basket, large canvas tote, or pop-up hamper handy for collecting and carrying used towels to the laundry room.

At the end of the season, deflate and store lightweight pool toys such as rafts in a lidded plastic container, a storage hammock strung up in a corner of the garage or basement, or an overhead ceiling rack.

(see also Storage Solutions, pages 153, 175)

Life is too short for clutter.

Give yourself permission
to let go of everything
that no longer serves a
purpose in your life.
Have courage.

Bank safe-deposit box

A bank safe-deposit box is ideal for valuable jewelry, rare coins, and other collectibles. It's also the best place to store original copies of certain legal and financial documents, such as:

- Marriage, birth, and death certificates
- Settlement and divorce papers
- Adoption, custody, and citizenship papers
- Diplomas
- Property deeds
- Motor vehicle titles
- Stock and bond certificates
- U.S. savings bonds and certificates of deposit
- Contracts, including mortgages, deeds, promissory notes, and other legally binding agreements
- Military papers
- Patents and copyrights
- Home inventory list, including photos of each room and purchase receipts
- Important data disks
- Any items you deem worthy of safekeeping

If you are the primary account holder, it's a good idea to add a secondary account holder who is authorized to open your box in the event that you are unable to do so. If, and only if, you do this, you may also store the originals of your will and trust papers. Do not store anything in a safe-deposit box that you may need to access in a hurry, such as passports, living wills, health care proxy, and powers of attorney.

You may be able to write off the cost of a safe-deposit box on your income tax returns if the contents include papers relating to income-producing property; check with your tax preparer. You may need a rider on your homeowner's or renter's policy to cover the contents of your safe-deposit box; check with your insurance agent.

An alternative to a safe-deposit box is a locking Underwriter's Laboratory (UL)–approved fire-resistant file cabinet or safe.

B

BELTS AND NECKTIES

Store belts and neckties so that you can remove one and return it without disturbing the others. Store neckties unknotted and in such a way that they won't wrinkle. While you can roll and store belts and neckties in a drawer, hanging them makes it quicker and easier to put away and retrieve them. An inexpensive solution is to count your belts and ties and tap that number of nails or small hooks into the wall, leaving a little room for additional purchases.

Ready-made organizers include wall- or door-mounted racks and special hangers that can hold several dozen belts or neckties; many are designed to store a combination of belts and ties. For a tight space, look for a valet rail that attaches to the outside of a closet-rod mount and slides in and out.

(see also Storage Solutions, pages 101, 224)

BICYCLES

Resting a bicycle against a wall is not a good way to store it, as it may be damaged if it accidentally tips over. Safer storage options range from inexpensive hooks and wall mounts to hang bicycles by the frame or a wheel to a pulley system that allows you to suspend them from the ceiling. Another option that works well is a floor-to-ceiling rack that can hold two bicycles.

BILLS, PAID

Unless they are tax-deductible business expenses, statements for cable, telephone, electric, garbage pickup, water, sewer, and other services and utilities can be shredded as soon as they are paid. There is no legal or tax reason to save these billing statements, as they do not prove payment. Your canceled check proves payment. And you can find the check number in your check register or on your bank statement.

If you are more comfortable saving utility statements, store them for one year only in a 13-pocket accordion file with 12 monthly pockets and a pocket for holding unpaid bills.

Even personal credit card statements don't *need* to be saved except to prove a business expense, in which case they should be stored with current-year tax documents. However, if you want to save credit card statements as proof of payment in lieu of a receipt, store them in a hanging folder labeled CREDIT CARDS with separate interior folders for each credit card. File in

B

ONE-MINUTE SOLUTION

Before filing bills to pay, make a note in your calendar to write and mail checks on a selected date in advance of the due date. Or schedule regular bill-paying days such as every Saturday or the first and fifteenth of every month. If you use an electronic calendar, add a reminder or use an electronic reminder service.

reverse chronological order (most current statement in front). Remove and shred statements at the end of each year or two or at your discretion.
(see also Storage Solutions, pages 15, 196)

Open bills where you pay them and you will be less likely to lose them.

23 percent of adults say they pay bills late (and thus **incur fees**) because they lose them. HARRIS INTERACTIVE SURVEY

B

BILLS, UNPAID

As bills arrive, either pay them immediately or store them in a designated holding place such as an accordion file or folder labeled Bills to Pay. Store only the bills and payment envelopes; toss the outer envelopes and any inserts.

Wherever you pay bills, designate a nearby drawer or cabinet shelf to store the "tools" you need to pay them, including check register, checks, envelopes, stamps, return-address labels, pen, calculator, and stapler. You also might want to keep a letter opener handy for opening bills. If you tend to pay bills at work or outside your home, consider setting up a portable bill-paying file with everything you need, including the unpaid bills.

Or you could go electronic: Online bill paying eliminates the need to file bills altogether. Have bills sent to you electronically and pay them online through each company's Web site. You also can set up bills to be paid automatically through your bank or bill-paying service directly to the phone company, utility company, or other entity.

You'll save on stamps and checks — and you'll save time, too. Another plus: Studies show that banking online can help decrease the risk of fraud and identity theft by more than 10 percent.

BIRDSEED

Store in a tightly sealed container to keep out hungry rodents. Empty bags into a recycled cat litter bucket with lid or a small metal trash can with tightly fitting lid. Label the container. Keep a scoop in or on top of the container for easy refilling of feeders.

BIRTH AND BAPTISMAL CERTIFICATES

Store original and certified copies in a safe-deposit box or fire- and burglar-resistant safe. (A baptismal certificate may be accepted as proof of birth in the absence of a birth certificate and in situations where the original birth was not recorded.)

(see also Storage Solutions, pages 15, 32)

BIRTHDAY AND ANNIVERSARY DATES

Never forget a birthday or anniversary again! There are many free birthday and anniversary reminder services available online. You can also enter important dates into the contact manager you use on your computer.

(continued)

Storage Solution

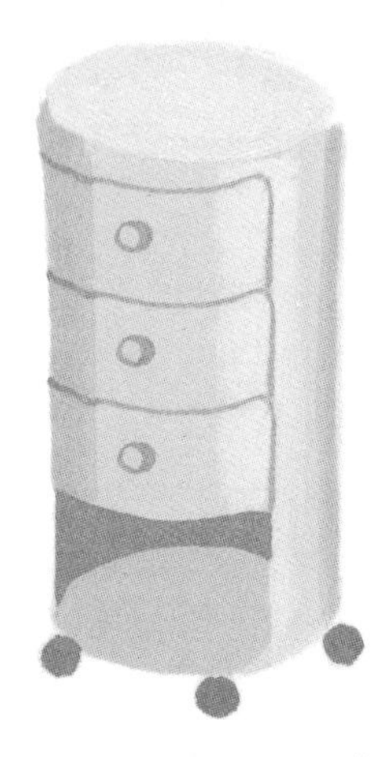

Mobile storage units

Do you need a portable storage system? Look for mobile filing carts, carts with drawers and shelves, and kitchen carts that you can store out of the way in closets or under desks and wheel out when you need them.

These units are also perfect for extra bathroom storage or for holding sewing and craft supplies, kids' toys, socks and underwear, and extra pantry foods. Tuck one into a corner of a closet for handy access to pet accessories, hats, and other items.

And there's the traditional way of recording birthdays and anniversaries, in a perennial birthday book for easy reference. You can also make notations on the appropriate dates in an annual calendar. At year end, transfer notations from one calendar to the next.

BLANKETS *(see Quilts/Comforters/Blankets)*

BLOUSES *(see Clothing: Blouses and shirts; Clothing, Out-of-Season)*

BLUEPRINTS AND OTHER PLANS

Roll up and store — individually or with related documents — in labeled cardboard tubes. If you've got a number of them that you need to access regularly, store rolled blueprints and plans (minus the tubes) in a mobile bin with tall compartments especially for rolled materials.

Or roll them up and store them in a cardboard wine or liquor box with divider inserts. Another option is to store blueprints and plans flat in stackable storage-shelf units made for this purpose or on an open shelf no taller than shoulder height.

BOATING GEAR *(see Sports Equipment and Gear)*

BOOKS

Organize books in a way that makes sense to you; after all, it's your collection. You might take a cue from libraries and bookstores, where nonfiction and fiction books are stored in different sections. Fiction is then arranged alphabetically by author. You could also organize by genre, such as historical fiction, romance, and mystery. Nonfiction books are typically organized by subject — gardening, parenting, travel. Use bookends as needed to create separate sections.

Arranging books so that the spines are aligned with the outer edge of the shelf will prevent dust from settling on shelf edges.

Keep children's books on the lower shelves or in bookcases in their rooms. Cookbooks are best stored in the kitchen, where they will be handy when needed.

An interesting alternative to book shelves (for paperbacks only) is a go-anywhere, invisible shelving system that creates the illusion of a line of books hanging unsupported on the wall. If you don't have space to display books, make a decision to give away the ones you will probably never read again or sell them to a used bookstore for cash or credit.

(see also Storage Solution, page 60)

ONE-MINUTE SOLUTION

I often use a stack of books, with spines facing out, as a bookend for a row of books. For visual interest, I like to mix books with other objects such as framed photographs, vases, and bowls.

BOOTS

Store wet or dirty boots on a plastic shoe tray near the entry. Clean and put away boots in the off-season.

Boot trees are the best way to retain the shape of boots and eliminate creasing. Trees feature an expanding bracket that provides the right amount of tension to keep boots standing while allowing air to circulate. Alternatively, you can stuff boots with tissue paper and cardboard forms. You can also purchase clear plastic stackable boxes made specifically for boots.
(see also Leather Items)

suitcases

- Infrequently used suitcases are a great way to store seasonal clothes and linens. Label the address tags with the contents or the owner of the clothes for quick identification.
- A hard-sided suitcase can hold holiday decorations.
- Tuck gifts and other surprises into a suitcase to foil snoopy kids and spouses.
- Stack two or three vintage suitcases to make a bedside table that also holds seasonal linens or infrequently used clothing items.
- Antique cosmetic cases make a charming container for jewelry, treasured letters and cards, and other special items.
- Smaller suitcases are great for yarn and fleece storage, as well as other crafts supplies.

You can buy gently used boxes online at a reasonable price, when and if you need them. Or check out one of the online communities where people give away stuff for free, such as Freecycle and Craigslist.

B

BOXES, CARDBOARD

If storage space is not an issue, go ahead and save all the boxes you want. But unless you have an immediate or foreseeable need for the boxes, such as an upcoming move or shipping a number of holiday gifts, the best place to store boxes in is your recycling bin. Store whatever boxes you decide to save in the attic or on high shelves or atop cabinets in the basement or garage. If space is limited, fold boxes flat, tie them together with twine, and tuck them away behind shelving or alongside cabinets.

Exception: You may want to save the original boxes and packing materials for electronics equipment such as stereos, televisions, computers, monitors, and printers as well as electronic games and keyboards. The original packaging provides maximum protection should you need to return an item by mail for warranty service or to transport it to a new home. Stack them in a corner of the attic or crawl space; if you must store them in the basement, put them on a pallet or a couple of 2×4s to keep them off the floor so they don't get damp.

BROCHURES AND FLYERS

Ask yourself: Do I really need to save this brochure or flyer — or just the pertinent information? Toss the paper whenever you can. File brochures you want to save so you can find them again. For example, you might set up a hanging file folder for TRAVEL & ENTERTAINMENT with interior folders labeled LOCAL, OUT-OF-TOWN, and VACATION for storing information about restaurants and places of interest.

(see also Local Area Information; Storage Solution, page 168)

As you think about where to store an object, ask yourself **where am I likely to look for it**, rather than where should I put it?

B

BULK FOOD AND PAPER ITEMS

If you have room in your everyday storage areas, you can store extra paper towels, toilet tissue, toiletries, canned goods, and other items there where they will be convenient when you need them. If not, designate a single space where you can store all the things you buy in bulk from your favorite wholesale store: in the garage or basement, laundry room, or an extra closet.

A freestanding shelving unit makes a good mouse- and moisture-proof storage space. Arrange it like a mini-store where you can go to replenish supplies. Consider removing multiple items, such as boxes of cereal or bottles of juice, from their outer packaging for easier access and to keep the bulk storage area neat and tidy.

(see also Toilet Tissue, Extra Rolls)

BUSINESS CARDS

If you save business cards, you need a simple way to store them so that you can find them again or at least find specific contact information. The simplest way is to scan the cards into your computer contact management program, such as Outlook or ACT. There are several scanners made specifically for this purpose.

ONE-MINUTE SOLUTION

If you use a card file book to store contact information for service providers, don't worry about alphabetizing or organizing the cards. Just add new ones as you get them and take a moment to remove cards you no longer need. Card file books are also a good way to store frequent buyer cards from your favorite stores.

Once scanned, there's no need to save the physical cards, as you will be able to sort and search contacts and even forward contacts to others via e-mail.

If you prefer to store the actual cards, there are a number of options. Card file books are useful for storing a relatively small number of business cards. You can have different books to separate types of contacts, such as household service providers and business contacts. Another option is a binder with protective pages designed to hold business cards and dividers to

B

sort alphabetically or by type. But if you want to file alphabetically, a business card file box is the simpler solution.

(see also Storage Solutions, pages 188, 196)

BUTTONS

Keep the spare buttons from new clothing in their original plastic or paper envelopes and either staple the sales tags to them or attach a label with a description of the items, such as "Ann Taylor navy jacket size 8." Keep them in a designated container (a clear plastic box or ziplock bag is a good choice) near your sewing supplies.

A clear plastic hardware drawer organizer is a great way to store a large stash of loose buttons. Organizing by color will make it easier to find just the right button.

If you don't mind going on a treasure hunt when you need a button, just toss them all into a lidded tin or jar or a ziplock bag and store them in a labeled bin or basket near your sewing supplies.

C

CAMERAS

Do not store in an extremely hot place such as in direct sunlight, near a heater, or in a car parked in the sun. Also, do not store cameras in extremely cold or humid places. When not in use, always store your camera in a camera case to protect it from sand, dust, liquid spills, and accidental bumping and falls.

CAMPING EQUIPMENT *(see Sports Equipment and Gear)*

CANCELED CHECKS

Since the federal Check 21 legislation took effect in 2004, most banks do not return canceled paper checks. Some banks provide imaging of recent canceled checks with online bank statements. Others include separate pages with images of written checks, which can be stored in a three-ring binder. In the absence of these copies, banks will provide substitute checks upon request.

So the question really is this: What do you do with that stash of canceled checks dating back to the days before check imaging? While canceled checks may be used as documentation to support your income tax

(continued)

Safe

A locking Underwriter's Laboratory (UL)–approved, fire-resistant file cabinet or safe is an alternative to a bank safe-deposit box and is certainly more convenient. But be aware that fire resistant does not mean fireproof. In high temperatures, paper may disintegrate and other contents may be damaged.

Canceled Checks *(continued)*
returns or as proof of payment, the Federal Reserve says bank statements are also acceptable as proof of payment. If you have corresponding statements, you can shred those canceled checks.

C

CANDLES

Do not store candles in your garage or attic, where excessive heat is likely to melt or warp them. Store candles in a cool, dark, dry place in your home, such as a linen or hall closet, away from any sources of heat, including heat generated by appliances, heat ducts, and household pipes.

Contrary to what you might have read or heard, candles should not be stored in the refrigerator or freezer. Excessive cold can crack them, and exposure to moisture can inhibit lighting. The best storage temperature is between 50 and 80°F (10–27°C). Avoid prolonged exposure to direct sunlight or fluorescent light, which can fade or discolor candles.

More tips:

» Store pillar and jar candles upright; tapers should be stored tapers flat to prevent bending if they become too warm.

(continued)

That which we persist in doing becomes easier — not that the nature of the task has changed, but our ability to do has increased.

RALPH WALDO EMERSON

Less is more. The less stuff you have, the less time and energy – and space – it takes to contain and maintain it all, freeing up more time, energy, and space for the pursuit of happiness.

Candles *(continued)*

- Prevent nicks and scratches by wrapping candles in tissue or paper toweling. Slide wrapped tapers into a paper towel roll for extra protection.
- Layer candles in a sturdy box or lidded plastic container with paper toweling between layers.
- Wrap scented candles with plastic wrap or put them into a ziplock bag to help retain the fragrance.
- Store birthday candles near other party supplies in a ziplock bag.

CAPS *(see Hats and Caps)*

CAR STUFF

Use the built-in storage compartments of your vehicle to organize various items by category. The glove compartment is a good place to store items that may be required from time to time, such as the owner's manual, vehicle registration, and proof of insurance, as well as emergency items such as a flashlight, some extra cash, a bottle of water, and perhaps some non-perishable food items such as crackers.

The console compartment is a better choice for storing items that you may need to reach while seated

C

in the front seat, such as sunglasses, cell phone, chargers, tissues, sanitizing gel or wipes, napkins, loose change, business cards, and a notebook and pen for jotting down messages, notes, and thoughts.

Door compartments are handy for storing a travel-sized umbrella, maps, directions, and perhaps guides to free wireless hotspots or local restaurants. The passenger's door compartment can hold a folded windshield sunscreen and additional items as needed.

There are a variety of vehicle-organizing products available, ranging from visor organizers for compact discs or receipts to organizers that hang behind the front seats to provide storage for children's games and toys. And don't forget that you need a place to put trash.

The trunk is essentially one big storage compartment. If your home had the same ratio of storage space to square footage as your car, I probably would not be writing this book!

Pop-up totes are a great item to store in your trunk to help you carry bags of groceries from the car to the house. A cooler or specially insulated bag will keep frozen items from thawing.

One of my favorite car organizers is a "sticky" pad that you place on the dash to keep your cell phone, iPod, sunglasses, and other items within reach. A special, cushy material holds items securely — even in a quick stop or turn — without magnets, clips, straps, or adhesives.

If you use your vehicle as a moving office, look for foldable seat and trunk organizers and ones that hang on the front of the passenger's seat to help keep you organized on the go. Consider keeping product brochures and flyers, client or project folders, samples, and promotional items in hanging file crates in the trunk. Lock crates together with Velcro strips or tie fasteners to keep them from moving around, and secure with a tie-down to keep them from tipping.

Storage Solution

Shelves and shelf dividers

Bookshelves aren't just for books. You can shelve CDs and DVDs, videotapes, audiotapes, magazines, photo albums and scrapbooks, games, toys, decorative items, and more. Add storage space to any room with free-standing book shelves or install a shelving system on any bare wall.

Maximize closet storage space by installing shelves from the clothes rod to the ceiling. Shop for do-it-yourself shelving systems that are strong enough to hold hundreds of pounds, yet flexible enough to be reconfigured as your needs change.

In kitchens and bathrooms, roll-out shelves make it easier to organize, store, and retrieve even those items at the back. You can buy a do-it-yourself kit at hardware and home stores. To organize items under the kitchen or bathroom sink, look for shelves with breakaway sections that fit around the plumbing.

Sliding baskets or clip-on under-shelf baskets can be used on shelves in a linen closet to organize a first-aid kit or stocks of soap and other toiletries. Another simple

solution is to put everything in long baskets or bins that you can pull out when you need to access the contents and then push back to store.

Freestanding shelves help maximize vertical storage space in cabinets. Clip-on shelf dividers will keep piles of sweaters, T-shirts, jeans, and linens from falling into each other and off the shelf.

Safety tip: Avoid storing heavy objects on upper shelves to ward off injury when retrieving them.

ONE-MINUTE SOLUTION

To reduce junk mail, register with the Direct Marketing Association Mail Preference Service and ask for your name to be removed from its members' mailing lists. To stop selected catalogs from coming, visit Catalog Choice online.

CAT SUPPLIES *(see Pet Paraphernalia)*

CATALOGS

Don't just let them pile up. Set up a catalog file. As soon as new catalogs arrive, either recycle them or store the ones you want in the file. Replace older catalogs with the newer issues. You also can keep catalogs with magazines and other material you plan

(continued)

What will you do with all the space you free up once you get organized? **Visualize it.** Believe it is possible. Then make it happen.

C

Catalogs *(continued)*

to read later. Use sticky notes or flags to mark pages with items of interest before filing.

Like magazines, it's best to store catalogs vertically so you can flip through them. Alphabetize if you want to. Alternatively, tear out pages with items you may want to purchase, staple them to the order form (or back cover with customer and source codes), and file them in a three-ring binder with divider tabs for various categories such as CLOTHING, HOME FURNISHINGS, and GIFTS. Label the binder.

(see also Magazines; Storage Solution, page 168)

CDS AND DVDS

A simple solution is to shelve CDs and DVDs as you would books. Consider organizing a small collection by category or alphabetize by artist. Organize a larger collection the way music stores do: first by category of music such as blues, jazz, or orchestra and then within category by name of artist. Use bookends to separate types of music.

Special storage boxes or slotted drawers that allow you to flip through your collection are another great option. You may want to find one large box that holds your entire collection or divide it into smaller boxes,

(continued)

“

The easiest way to find something lost around the house is to buy a replacement.

AUTHOR UNKNOWN

labeled by category. Before buying a ready-made organizer, count up how many CDs or DVDs you have so you know what you need.

I like the look of tower storage units, and they work well for small collections if your only goal is to store all your discs in one place, but I find them impractical for organizing collections. I once bought a CD tower and got it all organized alphabetically by artist, only to realize that to add new CDs I had to rearrange the whole thing. (I ended up giving it away.)

Ideally, your multimedia collection will be stored conveniently near your CD or DVD player. If lack of space dictates another solution, consider an underbed storage box or CD storage album that allows you to easily carry your collection, or a portion of it, from room to room or from home to car and back. In addition to portability, storage albums are an excellent space-saving option for compact discs.

If you're in the market for a new CD player, look for one with a CD changer that can store all your CDs, with features that allow you to select by artist, CD, or track. Be sure to store all CDs and DVDs at room temperature, away from direct sunlight and heat sources.
(see also Books; Storage Solution, page 60)

CHARGERS AND CABLES *(for cell phones, PDAs, MP3 players, digital cameras)*

Convenient as it may be, leaving chargers plugged in to the outlet is not a good idea; even when the charger is not attached to the device, it is drawing electrical power that you are paying for. An ideal solution is to purchase a charging station that can accommodate chargers for all of your electronic devices. Locate the charging station near an electrical outlet and plug the devices into a power strip hidden behind the station. Switch off the power strip when not in use.

Alternatively, consider designating one drawer for storing all chargers, preferably a drawer near an electrical outlet for easy access. You might use this drawer as the home base for other components such as cables and even the devices themselves.

Put the electronic item and all associated components into a clear plastic box (food-storage containers are perfect!) or ziplock bag. Label the boxes and bags so that you can easily find what you need, return items when not in use, and know what's missing if you see an empty box or bag. Labeled bags also make it easy to grab and go when traveling.

Another option is to store chargers and cables in the pockets of a hanging shoe organizer, provided you label the pockets.

CHRISTMAS DECORATIONS *(see Decorations, Seasonal)*

CITIZENSHIP PAPERS

Store in a bank safe-deposit box. Give a copy to the executor of your estate.

CLEANING TOOLS AND SUPPLIES

Pare down to the products and tools you love and use and get rid of everything else (following directions for disposal). Store all of your cleaning tools and supplies in one place and group by use. Utilize wall space with wall-mounted organizers for hanging mops, brooms, and long-handled dusters. Store clean rags and dust cloths in a hanging bag or basket on a shelf.

Maximize space within a utility closet by installing shelving or a door-mounted rack. You may even be able to build one. Just be sure you can open the door without the rack hitting the jamb and include a ledge or "railing" at the front of each shelf to keep items from falling off.

ONE-MINUTE SOLUTION

Consider temperature when deciding where to store cleaning supplies. The garage may not be a good option due to extremes of heat and cold. The compounds in car wax, for example, will undergo an irreversible chemical change when subjected to temperatures below freezing.

Consider storing basic cleaning supplies in a special caddy or bucket for easy carting from room to room. Or stash a supply of dusting cloths and cleaners in strategic spots around the home, such as behind books on a shelf, so if you get inspired to clean, you can dust off your books, polish the coffee table, or clean your leather sofa. Or keep some cleaning supplies in each bathroom for quick, everyday cleaning. Just be sure to keep all cleaning products out of reach of children and pets.

(see also Storage Solution, page 224)

C

Dressers

If possible, move your dresser into your clothes closet so that all of your clothes are together in one place. Designate dresser drawers for types of clothing such as underwear. Arrange clothing in drawers so you can easily see what's in them.

Dressers can also be used throughout your home to provide attractive freestanding storage.

- Place one in a hallway to store linens.
- Keep one in a bathroom for storing extra towels and supplies.
- Move an old one into the garage to store sports equipment and gear.
- A guest room dresser can hold out-of-season clothing or gift-wrapping supplies.

CLOTHING

Aim to fill your closet rods to no more than 75 percent capacity to make it easier to retrieve and rehang items. Choose hangers that slide smoothly, preferably pivoting hangers that make it easier to hang everything in the same direction. Group and hang like items together (pants, dresses, long-sleeved shirts, short-sleeved shirts).

If you want, you can arrange items within each group by color from light to dark and solid to patterns. Consider using labeled clothes rod dividers to create sections.

Add lighting if needed to ensure that your closet is well lit. Use shelf dividers to keep things like sweaters, jeans, and T-shirts neatly stacked. It's also helpful to have a valet pole to plan your wardrobe for the day or pack for a trip. Look for poles that hang over the clothes rod.

Blouses and shirts: Button the top button on shirts and blouses to prevent slipping from the hanger.

Coats and jackets: Hang on sturdy hangers. Button all buttons to keep jackets from sliding off hangers and prevent hanger marks. If you don't have

(continued)

THE HANGER TRICK

At the beginning of each new season or after organizing your closet, hang items with the hook facing you. **When you return worn or clean clothes to your closet, hang them the normal way with the hanger facing the wall.** At the end of the season, you will know exactly which items you wore and which you didn't, and that may help you decide which to donate.

ONE-MINUTE SOLUTION

Always wash clothing before storing. Perspiration, odors, and stains on natural fabrics attract hungry clothes moths, as does the use of fabric softener or starch. Avoid using mothballs in storage. Yes, they repel moths, but they're also toxic to breathe. Use cedar blocks or chips instead.

Clothing *(continued)*

a coat closet, a freestanding coat rack in the front entrance is a great place to store everyday coats as well as guests' coats. You also can use a freestanding coat rack in your bedroom or walk-in closet to temporarily hang clothes you plan to wear again.

Dresses: Invest in padded hangers to protect the shoulders of your dresses. Store formal wear and holiday dresses in fabric garment bags in the back of your closet or in a spare closet. Use a skirt hanger to clamp

C

the top of a strapless or spaghetti-strap dress; fold a washcloth over the fabric to protect against marks.

Exercise and gym clothing: Fold exercise clothing into small squares that can be "filed" upright in rows. Or roll these items instead of folding them.

Pajamas: When I was a kid, my mother taught me to "store" my pajamas under my pillow when I got dressed. As an adult, I hang them on a hook in my closet if I plan to wear them again soon. (The back of the bathroom door is another convenient spot.)

But I still think that under-the-pillow pajama storage is a neat idea. At least you won't have to listen to your children wailing, "I can't find my pajamas."

Pants and jeans: Do you hang them or fold them? How you store pants is as much a matter of personal preference as of space. Removing pants from the dryer slightly damp and hanging from the cuffs can help prevent wrinkling. Zip the zipper and fasten the top button.

You can hang pants or jeans in one of three ways:

1) Open and hung from the waist

2) Folded lengthwise and hung from the cuff

3) Folded over a hanger

(continued)

Storage Solution

Vacuum-seal storage bags

If you're pressed for space, consider vacuum-packing blankets, coats, sweaters, and other bulky seasonal items. Look for specially designed space-saving storage bags that are sealed with the aid of a vacuum cleaner to reduce total volume by up to 75 percent. These inexpensive bags protect the contents from dust and dirt as well as insects and rodents.

Store sealed bags on a closet shelf, under a bed, or inside a suitcase. Hanging, space-saving bags are great for storing coats and other items on hangers.

Note: Do not use to store vellum blankets, leather, fur, or down comforters and pillows.

Jeans and permanent-press pants can also be folded in thirds and stacked on a closet shelf or in a drawer.

Scarves: I fold and hang large or heavy scarves on individual pant/skirt hangers with clips. You can also use multitiered pant or skirt hangers or hang them on a belt or tie organizer. Another idea is to store them in lidded plastic storage containers on a closet shelf or in a drawer.

Hang winter scarves from pegs or hooks in the entryway closet or on the back of a door or store them in a designated basket or container on a shelf. Keep the one you wear most often with the coat that it matches.

Shorts: Hang in your closet from skirt or pant hangers or store flat or folded in a drawer.

Skirts: Hang unfolded from the waist on skirt hangers.

Socks and panty hose: Designate a drawer (or two if necessary) for socks. Fold socks into thirds or simply roll them and "file" in rows in a drawer by type and/or color.

You can also organize and store hosiery in a shoe bag organizer or use shoe boxes to keep them sorted in a drawer.

ONE-MINUTE SOLUTION

One homemade solution I've always loved for small, lightweight scarves is to hook several shower rings together and hang one ring over the neck of a hanger. Then you can thread the scarves through the rings for easy visibility and access.

Hate folding socks? Drawer dividers can help to keep socks organized; one style in particular eliminates the need to fold — just stuff each pair into its own cube. Pinning together mates with a plastic clothespin before tossing them into the hamper eliminates the need for matching up after washing and you can just put them away as is. You can also buy special sock clips (also called sock rings or organizers) that let you color-code socks by family member for easier sorting and fewer cases of missing socks.

(continued)

Getting rid of clutter eliminates 40 percent of housework in the average home.

SOURCE: NATIONAL SOAP & DETERGENT ASSOCIATION

Clothing *(continued)*

Suits: You can hang suits as suits (on a suit hanger) or as separates. Many fashion consultants recommend hanging the pieces separately so you don't forget that you can mix and match suit jackets and pants or skirts.

Sweaters: Do not hang. Fold and store flat in stacks on a shelf or in a drawer. In a drawer, arrange from left to right with one sweater overlapping the next, so you can see them all.

T-shirts: Fold and stack on a shelf or in a drawer. In a drawer, arrange from left to right with one T-shirt overlapping the next, so you can see them all. Or roll and fold.

Underwear: To fold or not to fold? It's up to you. You can toss all your underwear into a drawer or bin on a shelf and call it good. Or you can take it to the other extreme and use drawer dividers to store by type or color or fold as described for exercise clothing (page 74). You can also organize and store in a shoe bag organizer.

(see also Clothing, Out-of-Season; Storage Solutions, pages 60, 101, 224)

C

Tickler file

The tickler file solves the problem of what to do with papers that you will need on a specific date. I was introduced to this simple tool early in my professional career and like many everyday users, I swear by it. You can file items such as tickets, travel itineraries, party invitations, event flyers, bills to be paid, claim stubs for dry cleaning and repairs to be picked up, copies of rebate claims in process or orders placed online, estimated tax forms, and birthday cards to mail.

You also can file papers associated with upcoming meetings or projects and follow-up reminders and things to do such as change the smoke-detector batteries and the furnace filter.

The tickler file is basically a paper sorter. I use a set of two hanging file folders with 31 interior folders labeled 1-31 for days and 12 folders labeled with the months of the year. Here's how it works: If you have a bill due on the 15th of the month, file it in the folder or slot labeled 15. If it's a paper you need a few months from now, file it in the appropriate-month folder. At the end of each month, move the next month's papers into the appropriate daily folders. The key to making this system work is to get into the habit of checking the tickler file each day.

You can make your own tickler file or find ready-made solutions (also known as file sorters) at office supply stores. The most popular, ready-made version is an accordion-fold book with either A–Z or 1–31 dividers. If you're using file folders, keep them in a filing cabinet drawer within arm's reach of your office chair or in a rolling file cart or desktop organizer that holds hanging files. The book-style tickler file can be stored on a shelf, in a desktop step sorter, or in a desk drawer.

gift or shopping bags

- Sturdy gift bags or boutique shopping bags (the heavy, laminated kind are best) are pretty and offer a simple and unique way to store file folders on an open shelf.
- You can also use them to stash catalogs or reading material on a shelf.
- Use one large gift bag to store others, folded flat. Store wrapping accessories or gifts to be wrapped.
- Use a pretty gift or shopping bag as a tote bag for books and videos to return.
- Store several large ones in your car to reuse as shopping bags.
- They can hold large spools of ribbon, string, and twine, as well as yarn, fabric, and other craft materials.
- Use one to hold personal supplies such as electric hair clippers with all the attachments or a manicure/pedicure kit; stash the bag in a closet or under the bathroom sink when not in use.
- A small bag can make a handy trash container for the car or can hold a water bottle, tissue box, hand wipes, and so on.

CLOTHING, CHILDREN'S

A flexible storage system with movable brackets or shelves that can be easily removed and repositioned allows you to reconfigure your storage area to grow with your child. Use shelf dividers to keep things like sweaters, jeans, and T-shirts neatly stacked. Store by size on labeled shelves or in labeled drawers. Hang a second, lower rod so that even small children can reach and hang up their everyday clothes. Store dressy outfits and less frequently worn clothing on the upper rod. Use children's hangers for children's clothing.

CLOTHING, OUT-OF-SEASON

Move out-of-season clothing off to one side of your closet rod, or to another closet or storage space if you have one. The storage space should be clean, dry, and airy with no direct sunlight. If your basement or attic is climate controlled, you can set up a hanging rack or mobile closet to store seasonal garments. Another option is to purchase large garment boxes with rods from a local moving company.

Sweaters and almost everything else should be folded and put in covered containers. If you have a cedar chest, great. Lidded plastic storage bins also protect clothing and bedding from dust, insects, and

C

rodents. If in-home storage space is limited, keep items in containers that will fit under a bed. If you need a little extra space, raise the height of your bed with risers and add an extra-long bed skirt to hide under-bed storage bins.

(see also Leather items; Storage Solutions, pages 75, 153)

COATS AND JACKETS *(see Clothing: Coats and jackets)*

COMFORTERS *(see Quilts/Comforters/Blankets)*

COMIC BOOKS

Store in binders in plastic protective sheets. Use archival-quality sheets for vintage and collectible comic books.

(see also Magazines; Storage Solution, page 168)

COMPUTER SUPPLIES *(see Office/School Supplies)*

COSMETICS

Store everyday items such as makeup and cleansers in a bag, basket, or other portable container that is easy to take out and put away. Choose a container that will store all your makeup *and* fit neatly into its storage space. Store in a drawer or cabinet near where you apply your makeup. Keep away from direct sunlight and excessive heat.

(see also Toiletries)

COUPONS

You can buy ready-made organizers with dividers or slots for grocery store coupons — or make your own from a check file or small accordion-style folder. Save only those coupons you are likely to use before the expiration date. Some people store their grocery coupons in their vehicles; that never worked for me. I store my coupon file in my kitchen because that's where I plan my shopping. Then I take with me to the store only the coupons I need.

On the other hand, I do carry non-grocery coupons and gift certificates in a plastic envelope in my purse. You may want to have two coupon organizers — one for grocery items and one for all other coupons, sorted by store category such as clothing, furnishings, services. Get into the habit of tossing expired coupons when filing new coupons.

C

CRAFTS *(see Arts and Crafts Supplies; Handicraft Projects)*

CREDIT CARDS

Carry in your wallet only those cards that you really need; leave all others at home in a locked filing cabinet.
(see also Wallet Items; Storage Solution, page 15)

CREDIT REPORTS

Save with other personal information in a locked filing cabinet or other safe place in your home. Keep only the most recent. Shred old reports.
(see also Storage Solutions, pages 15, 188)

CUPS AND MUGS

If you keep your cups and mugs in a cabinet, screw hooks underneath the shelves to hang them from. Or look for an over-the-shelf cup holder or stacking shelf to add an extra layer of storage.

Or hang everyday mugs from hooks underneath a cabinet near the coffeemaker. You can also find freestanding coffee mug trees to store frequently used mugs in the open.

Store delicate and heirloom teacups and saucers in quilted china storage boxes.

D

DEATH CERTIFICATES

Store originals and any certified copies in a locked filing cabinet or bank safe-deposit box.

DECORATIONS, SEASONAL

Store decorations by season in stackable plastic containers with lids. Cardboard is okay, but plastic offers better protection from dirt, insects and rodents, water, and other potential damage. Clear plastic is always a good idea but you can also choose different colors for different seasons or bins with different-color lids. Label the front of every bin and all four sides while you're at it, so you can turn and rearrange boxes if needed.

You may want to number boxes and create a master index of stored items that includes the box number where they are stored and location of the box. You can do this on a spreadsheet and store it on your computer and/or in a storage area to make it easy to find specific items.

If space allows, designate a single location for storage of seasonal decorations. Store bins so that the upcoming season's decorations are most accessible. That means moving those bins toward the front or

(continued)

“

Success is the sum of small efforts, repeated day in and day out . . .

ROBERT J. COLLIER

egg cartons

- Protective foam egg cartons are perfect for storing small holiday tree ornaments, especially delicate ornaments.
- They are also good for sorting buttons and beads or small hardware supplies.
- Children can paint cardboard ones in bright colors and use them to sort tiny treasures.
- Reuse foam ones as painting trays or the paper kind to sprout seedlings.
- Egg cartons can be cut to fit in a desk drawer with as many units as you need to hold paper clips, thumbtacks, and other supplies.

top of your storage area when putting away the most recent decorations, which should be stored at the bottom of the stack or at the back.

Pack holiday decorations and ornaments as if you might be moving because . . . well, you never know. Put away items in the reverse order that you will need them next year. For example, pack the Christmas tree lights on top of the garlands and ornaments.

Ornaments: Invest in a couple of sturdy, stackable ornament boxes with dividers. Or use a cardboard wine box and wrap fragile ornaments in tissue paper. It's best to store special keepsake ornaments in the original packaging for maximum protection.

Another method for storing fragile ornaments is to put a layer of shredded paper in the bottom of a box. Don't use newspaper — the ink makes a mess. Add a layer of ornaments, making sure they aren't touching, and then another layer of paper, and continue, finishing with a thick layer of paper on top.

You may want to store ornaments in boxes by type of ornament such as fabric, wood and metal, and glass.

Lights: To keep holiday lights from tangling, wrap strands around a piece of cardboard, starting with the connector end and finishing with the plug. Tuck the plug under a string to secure it. Avoid having to figure out which light strings go where by labeling the cardboard with a description, such as mantel or tree. Wrap with tissue or packing paper to protect against breakage and store in a box with other holiday decorations. If lights are the first holiday decorations you put up, store them at the top of the box or in a separate box stored on top of the others for easy access. Reel-type organizers are highly recommended for easy storage of lights, especially for long strings.

Artificial tree: I find it tedious to set up and dismantle an artificial tree. That's why I recommend plastic tree storage bags. You put the tree into the bag, zip it up, and carry it to your garage, basement, or attic. When the holidays come around, just carry it back into the house, unzip the bag, and pull out a ready-to-decorate or even partially decorated tree! Yes, it requires a little more storage space, but if you've got the room, this is a real timesaver. And unlike the original cardboard box, the plastic bag protects against dust as well as insect and rodent infestation.

Wall-mounted organizers

Make good use of vertical storage space. You can find wall-mounted organizers to hang everything from brooms and mops in the utility room, to cooking utensils and spices in the kitchen, to bicycles in the garage.

D

ONE-MINUTE SOLUTION

Before you take down seasonal decorations, take some photos so you can remember how you decorated your home last year. Store the photos with your decorations — be sure to put them on top!

Wreaths: Place artificial wreaths in a special wreath box or bag with tissue paper or newspaper lightly stuffed around them to help preserve their shape and store them lying flat. Or cover wreaths securely with a trash bag and hang on a wall in your seasonal storage area.
(see also Storage Solution, page 153)

DEEDS

Store in a fire- and burglar-resistant safe or in a safe-deposit box; may be discarded 10 years after property is sold. Cemetery deeds should be kept forever. Give a copy to your heir(s).

(see also Storage Solution, page 32)

DIPLOMAS

Store originals in a bank safe-deposit box or fire- and burglar-resistant safe. If you would like to display them, frame and hang copies.

DISHES

Store everyday dishes on shelves in a cabinet near the dishwasher or your table — whatever makes it easier for you to put them away and retrieve them. You can buy special dividers to store dishes in drawers if that is more convenient.

Special-occasion and heirloom dishes should be stored in china storage boxes with cushioned dividers between plates.

DIVORCE DECREE

Store original in your bank safe-deposit box.

DOG STUFF *(see Pet Paraphernalia)*

DONATIONS

Keep a donations box in a central location in your home into which you and other family members can toss items to be given to charity, including clothing, electronic equipment, games, toys, and books. Keep a running list, including detailed description (brand name, color, size), of the items you put in the box and approximate second-hand value. When the box gets full, take it to the charity of your choice. Staple your list to the receipt and file with your current-year tax records.

A very effective technique with children is to put a donation box in each child's room and give them a choice: either put their things away or toss them into the donation box.

DRESSES *(see Clothing: Dresses)*

DVDS *(see CDs and DVDs)*

E

EARRINGS

There are several interesting ways to store earrings besides the traditional jewelry box. The earring tree is one solution that allows you to see all of your earrings at once. If you like that idea but need more storage space, a folding acrylic earring screen could be the answer. Also look for commercial jewelry display racks designed for earrings.

One simple solution that's not so pretty but very functional is to store pairs of earrings in ice cube trays. You can line a drawer with the trays or stack them for additional storage.

A piece of mesh hardware cloth (like chicken wire) stapled to a wooden frame provides a fun place to hang dangly earrings.

(see also Jewelry)

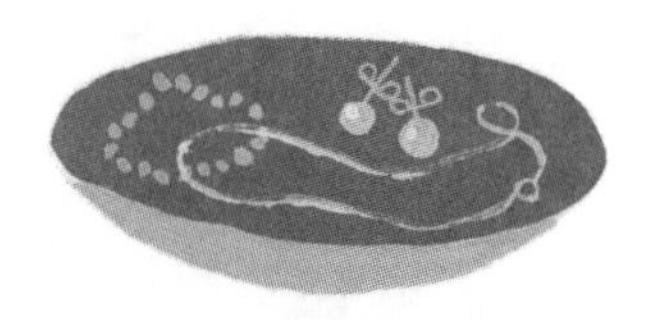

Sometimes, the best place
to store stuff is . . .
a. in other people's homes
(**donate it**) or
b. in the garbage or
recycling bin (**toss it**).

ELECTRONIC STORAGE *(see Storage Solution, page 196)*

EMERGENCY CONTACTS

Program emergency numbers into your telephone and be sure every member of your household knows how to make emergency calls. Alternatively, pin a list to a bulletin board or tape it to the inside of a cabinet door near the phone.

E

E-TICKETS *(see Tickets)*

EXERCISE AND GYM CLOTHING *(see Clothing: Exercise and gym clothing)*

EXTENSION CORDS

Store all cords in one place, such as a junk drawer or garage cabinet, so you always know where to find one when you need it. Wrap each cord to about the same size and tuck the end under to secure it or secure it with a twist tie or rubber band. You may want to store them in ziplock bags or empty toilet tissue rolls, labeled by length.

(see also Storage Solution, page 267)

Drawer dividers

Adjustable dividers in kitchen and bathroom drawers are ideal for sorting and organizing the contents, especially in large drawers. A cutlery tray can also be put to use for this purpose, or look for separate units in various sizes that interlock and can be arranged to suit your needs.

Ziplock bags are another simple storage solution for containing small items of similar types in a junk drawer.

(see also Storage Solution, page 267)

E

EYEGLASSES AND SUNGLASSES

In a recent survey of my readers, eyeglasses were one of the most frequently misplaced items. Keep a spare pair of eyeglasses in your car if you need them for driving or in your nightstand drawer if you need them for reading. Store extra pairs of reading glasses in one designated place such as a drawer or basket, or in places where you are likely to need them, such as your briefcase or purse, living room, or kitchen.

If you frequently misplace your eyeglasses, consider attaching a lanyard, eyeglass chain, or necklace to at least one pair.

Donate used prescription eyeglasses and prescription or nonprescription sunglasses to the Lions Recycle for Sight Program or to the Gift of Sight Foundation. Look for a drop-off box at your eye doctor's office or the retail store where you shop for eyeglasses. The glasses will be shipped to regional recycling centers, where they will be cleaned, categorized by prescription, and prepared for distribution to needy people around the world.

FABRIC

Store new yardage by color. Fold each piece to the same size with the folded edges out in the same way that you would fold linens. Stack material on open shelves or in wire-mesh cubes to separate colors.

Sort remnants and scraps of material by color, and then fold pieces to uniform sizes. For example, if you have fat quarters (18- by 24-inch/46 by 61 cm pieces) for quilting, fold them in quarters and then in half again lengthwise. Fold smaller pieces to the same size. Stack the fabric with the folded edges facing in the same direction. Then stand the pieces with folded ends up in clear plastic bins. If your bins measure 11 by 15 inches (28 by 38 cm), you will be able to create two side-by-side rows of fabric. Label the bins by color or pattern and stack them on a shelf.

Make a decision to toss or donate small scraps that you will probably never use. If you do have a use for the smaller scraps, fold and file them in an accordian-style folder with divided pockets — the kind of folder more frequently used to store bills or coupons. Store upright on a shelf or flat in a drawer.

FILM

Read the package label and follow storage instructions specific to the type of film. Do not store unprocessed film (or a loaded camera) in drawers or closets where you keep clothing or fabric, as these materials attract insects that can damage film.

Generally, it's best to store unused film in the original package under refrigeration. Allow several hours to one day for the package to warm up to room temperature before opening, to prevent condensation on the surface of the film. Use by the "Develop by" date for best results. Refrigerating or freezing does not extend that date. Avoid exposure to direct sunlight or temperatures above 70°F (21°C). Keep unused film in an insulating bag at higher temperatures.

When traveling by air, store unused high-speed film (800 ISO or higher) in your carry-on bag, where it can be easily removed to avoid potential damage by X-ray equipment. Unprocessed film may be stored for a few days under refrigeration in a sealed container. Allow container to return to room temperature before opening. When traveling, consider bringing along special mail-in envelopes that you can use to send off film for processing.

Storage Solution

Off-site storage

There are times when it makes sense to rent public storage space. You may, for example, need to temporarily store belongings if you are remodeling or selling your house or are between homes. You may want to store some furnishings and things to help your children establish their first homes as you downsize to a smaller, more affordable home. And of course, if you live in a small apartment or mobile home, you may need additional storage for seasonal or infrequently used items.

How much storage space do you need? Probably less than you think. A 5-foot-by-5-foot-by-8-foot (1.5 by 1.5 by 2.4 m) self-storage unit can hold a bicycle, trunk, wardrobe, and as many as three dozen boxes. A 5-foot-by-10-foot-by-8-foot (1.5 by 3.0 by 2.4 m) unit can hold the contents of a one-bedroom apartment.

You may be able to rent a portable or mobile storage unit that is delivered to your home, where you can pack it up at your leisure. When you're ready, the storage company will move the storage unit to its facility or to your new home.

Do insure your belongings, because the storage facility is not liable for theft, fire, or other disasters. Don't

count on your homeowner's insurance for coverage; most policies will pay only 10 percent of a claim for items stored away from home for an extended period.

Ideally, the storage facility you choose will have a computerized entry system and closed-circuit camera surveillance. You'll need a padlock and key; bringing your own will be less expensive than buying them from the storage facility. If you need regular access to your belongings, be sure to select a storage facility with convenient hours.

There are typically no long-term contracts for self-storage or portable storage — just a month-to-month agreement and a security fee that may or may not be refundable. The cost is higher for a climate-controlled unit with heat or air-conditioning, which is advisable for upholstered items, documents, electronic equipment, framed artwork, and other valuables.

FIREPLACE/WOODSTOVE SUPPLIES

You can buy containers and hangers specifically designed to store wood, kindling, and fire equipment such as pokers and bellows. Attractive alternatives include a sturdy basket, a heavy copper or brass bucket or bin, and a wooden box or small half-barrel — look around at flea markets and antique stores for something that matches your decor.

FOOD-STORAGE CONTAINERS

It makes sense to store leftover containers with food wraps since they serve the same function. To store the empty containers, nest together ones of the same shape and size. Store lids in one big container or basket. Or store all containers and lids in a large drawer.

Note: Some newer containers have interlocking lids or lids that snap to the bottom of the containers, so you don't have to flip your lid looking for lids and your cabinets stay organized.

If you need a new set (hey, they don't last forever), look for containers that are durable enough to go from freezer to microwave to dishwasher, yet inexpensive enough to give away to guests. Plastic deli and take-out containers can be reused a number of times (most are

ONE-MINUTE SOLUTION

The next time you pick up a pizza ask for a couple of clean pizza boxes that you can use to store quilt blocks and fabric remnants. Organize and label boxes according to color and stack them on a shelf. Pizza boxes are also handy for storing children's artwork, craft papers, a collection of postcards and note cards, or awards and ribbons from school and sports competitions.

dishwasher safe, but don't put them in the microwave). Or consider investing in collapsible storage containers.

FREQUENT FLYER CARDS

Some cards such as library cards, bus passes, and punch cards must be presented at the time of service. But if you don't need to present the actual card, as is the case with frequent flier cards and other memberships, type a list of the account numbers on a credit-card size paper, laminate it, and keep that in your wallet. Store the list on your computer and keep an extra copy in a file folder. You don't need to save the cards.

You may want to create one card for frequent flier numbers and one for frequent shopper accounts. It's a good idea to also include Customer Service telephone numbers for each account.

(see also Business Cards; Wallet Items)

FURS

Never, ever store fur in plastic. During the winter, hang fur coats on wide-shouldered hangers in cloth garment bags with plenty of room, so air can circulate and the fur won't get crushed. It's best to store fur away from light to prevent a change in color.

At the end of the wearing season, have your coats cleaned and stored by a professional furrier. Professional fur storage will prevent skins from drying out, protect from insect damage, and keep furs looking beautiful. Fur vaults are set at the optimal temperature and humidity: between 40 and 50°F (4–10°C) with humidity between 45 and 55 percent.

If you must store fur at home, be sure to store away from heat and moisture. Deter moths with cedar chips, not mothballs, which leave a strong odor that is difficult to remove, or store items in a cedar closet.

ONE-MINUTE SOLUTION

Simplify your life by buying the same type of gift for baby and bridal showers, birthdays, and other special occasions. Keep them near all your gift-wrapping supplies. Having a stash of greeting cards for various occasions is handy as well.

G

GAMES/PUZZLES

Store stacked on shelves or in a large drawer. If game boxes have deteriorated beyond repair, label the backs of the game boards and stack them vertically. Store game pieces in ziplock bags labeled to match the game board. Store the bags in a box labeled GAMES.

Puzzle pieces can be stored similarly. Cut the picture from the box and then label a ziplock bag for storing the puzzle pieces. Clip the bag to the picture with a binder clip.

GARDENING EQUIPMENT, TOOLS, AND SUPPLIES

Create a zone in your garage or in a storage shed for storing gardening equipment, tools, and supplies. When deciding where to store power equipment such as mowers and snowblowers, make it easy to get them in and out.

» Hang long-handled tools such as rakes and hoes on the wall. (See page 127.)

» Put frequently used hand tools, gloves, and other items in a bucket with a handle that you can tote to the garden.

» Store heavy bags of potting soil or fertilizer on shelves just below waist height, if possible.

» Put seasonal items such as vegetable stakes and cages and lighter items on higher shelves.

(see also Storage Solutions, pages 93, 224)

G

GIFTS FOR GIVING

Choose a single place to store gifts purchased in advance. Label a bin GIFTS and store it in a closet or spare room. If you purchased the gift for someone in particular, tape or pin a note to the gift with that person's name and the date of the event. If you have to hide gifts from curious recipients in your home, create and keep a list of the gifts in a Word document or spreadsheet along with the location of each item.

GIFT-WRAPPING PAPER AND ACCESSORIES

The ideal solution is to store wrapping paper together with gift bags, boxes, tissue paper, tape, scissors, bows, ribbons, and gift tags so you will have everything you need in one place. There are lots of organizing products available — everything from hanging organizers to under-bed containers to gift-wrapping stations.

Other storage solutions include an empty dresser drawer in a guest room; use the flat top of the dresser as a convenient place to wrap gifts. Many people store wrapping paper in a bedroom or hall closet. You can store paper rolls upright in a cardboard wine or liquor box with dividers or in a wine rack placed on a deep shelf. To keep wrapping paper from unwrapping, cut a slit from end to end in an empty wrapping tube and slide it over the new roll; it also makes a handy gift-wrap dispenser.

You can fold sheets of wrapping paper and tissue paper over the rods of a tiered pant hanger; slide rolls of ribbon over the top rod (secure with a clothespin at one end to keep rolls from falling off!) and hang

(continued)

Donna's Top 10 Storage Strategies

1. Box it
2. Bind it
3. Shelve it
4. Mount it

5. Hang it

6. Build it
7. Bag it
8. File it
9. Roll it
10. Hide it

Storage Solution

Built-in storage

Although it can be expensive, built-in storage can help increase the value of your home while making the best use of existing space. If you're handy, you can save money by doing it yourself. In addition to built-in bookcases, custom closets are a popular project. It's amazing how much you can store with a combination of single and double rods to accommodate short and long hanging items, plus built-in drawers (including jewelry drawers), shoe cubbies, sliding pant racks, and additional shelving to the ceiling.

Shop for furniture with built-in storage space — a lidded ottoman or bench, an entertainment center with media storage, a coffee table with drawers to store remote controls, or an office armoire with a place for the computer and storage spaces with doors to hide office supplies.

Look for ways to create storage space out of currently wasted space. For example, if you have a staircase in your home, you may be able to build shelves or drawers that take advantage of the hidden space underneath. Drawers could be used to store toys and games, wrapping paper and ribbon, hats, or slippers. A window seat can offer extra storage as well as a spot to curl up with a good book.

Gift-Wrapping Paper and Accessories *(continued)*
folded gift bags from the bottom rod, organized by size. Store bows in a gift bag or box on a shelf.
(see also Storage Solutions, pages 70, 224)

GLASSWARE

Store glasses upside down on a clean shelf (preferably covered with a washable liner) to keep the rims dust-free. Ideally, glasses will be stored near the refrigerator, dishwasher, or table for ease of serving or putting away and/or setting the table.
(see also Stemware)

GLOVES AND MITTENS

If you have just one pair, keep them in the pockets of the coat you wear most often. Otherwise, store them in a basket or storage container on a shelf in a closet or near the door or in a hanging shoe bag organizer with clear plastic pockets.
(see also Clothing, Out-of-Season; Storage Solutions, pages 101, 224)

G

ONE-MINUTE SOLUTION

Before putting away holiday decorations, it's become a ritual for me to recycle holiday greeting cards into unique gift tags. While watching TV or chatting on the phone, I grab a pair of scissors and see how many tags I can create from each card. I store these tags in an envelope tucked in with my other gift-wrapping materials.

GREETING CARDS AND LETTERS, RECEIVED

Choose the most meaningful ones — the ones that really touched your heart or came from the special people in your life — and store in a memorabilia box with other favorite memories. Or store your special cards and letters expressing love, thanks, or congratulations in a folder or album that you can pull out when you need to lift your spirits. You could also display cards on the branches of a photo mobile stand, a

G

freestanding metal tree that will hold dozens of cards clipped to its hanging branches. I tape special cards to the inside doors of my kitchen cabinets, where I can reread them frequently.

Consider scanning a large collection of cards into your computer and use a photo-organizing program to create albums for card types such as holiday, congratulations, and birthday, or organize them by sender.
(see also Memorabilia; Storage Solution, page 188)

GREETING CARDS, TO SEND

Purchase a greeting card organizer or make your own with a shoebox and cardboard dividers or index cards. Organize cards by occasion such as congratulations, thank you, and sympathy.

You may also want to create sections for each month where you can store cards you've preselected for upcoming birthdays, anniversaries, weddings, graduations, and other occasions. Address and store cards in the appropriate month with the date to send penciled on the envelope in the postage stamp area.

Or send real paper greeting cards from your computer through an online service and eliminate the need to store cards.
(see also Storage Solution, page 80)

ONE-MINUTE SOLUTION

Ask your dry cleaner if he accepts hanger returns. Store hangers to be recycled in a bag where you also "store" items to be dry-cleaned.

HAIR ACCESSORIES

What's a good way to store all those barrettes, clips, ribbons, ponytail holders, and headbands? A simple solution is to find a pretty basket or wooden box large enough to accommodate them all; look for one divided into several sections for sorting types. Another idea is to hang a length of ribbon on a wall and attach clips and barrettes to it. A clear plastic jewelry organizer or shoe bag organizer provides yet another solution.
(see also Jewelry; Storage Solution, page 224)

H

HANDBAGS *(see Purses)*

HANDICRAFT PROJECTS (KNITTING, EMBROIDERY, SEWING)

Keep current works in progress in a tote bag or basket, along with all the necessary materials and tools.

HANGERS

Store empty hangers together on a clothes rod. When you remove clothing from a hanger, move the hanger to the holding area. Sort them by type (pants, shirt, or padded) to make it easier to find the right hanger.

Keep a reasonable number of hangers in your closet; store extras in a hall closet, guest room, or other bedroom closets. Or keep them in the laundry room for drip-dry clothing and to hang items as you remove them from the dryer.

HARDWARE *(see Tools and Hardware)*

HATS AND CAPS

Store brimmed hats flat on a shelf or in hatboxes or storage containers to keep them dust-free. Store knitted hats in drawers or in containers on shelves.

Hang a large collection of baseball-type caps on a special cap organizer that hangs from a clothes rod or on the back of a door or a wall. To store just a few, hang on a hat rack or coat pegs. Avoid stacking hats and caps to protect their shape.
(see also Storage Solution, page 224)

HEALTHCARE PROXY

Also known as a medical directive, a copy of the health-care proxy should be stored in a fire- and burglar-resistant safe or bank safe-deposit box. Also give a copy to a close family member and to your doctor. Have your attorney keep the original. Shred papers that have been revised. *(see also Storage Solution, page 32)*

HOLIDAY DECORATIONS *(see Decorations, Seasonal)*

HOUSEHOLD INVENTORY

If you have an itemized list of household items for insurance purposes, store it along with documentary photos or videotape, receipts, and appraisals in a bank safe-deposit box, where it will be safe in the event of fire, theft, or other disaster. Be sure to include model, make, and serial number of appliances and electronic items. Give a copy to your insurance agent.

To:
From:

IDEAS

A simple way to capture and store ideas is to create a new Task folder in Outlook labeled Ideas. Delete the due date field. Enter ideas in the subject field. You can even attach (insert) e-mail items and files.

INSURANCE POLICIES

File only policies that are currently in effect. Shred all other policies, including those written for items you no longer own. Store at home in a locking filing cabinet. Create a hanging folder labeled Insurance and within that folder, insert interior folders for the various types of insurance: AUTO, HOME, LIFE.

INVITATIONS

Respond right away if required. Enter the time and location of the event on your calendar, along with any other pertinent details. If you can't RSVP immediately or you need to buy a gift, make a note on the calendar to do that or set an electronic reminder.

If you decide not to attend, or if you have all the information you need written on your calendar, toss the invitation. Take a moment to record or check the return address for accuracy in your address book

(continued)

coffee cans and other tins

- Wrapped with contact paper or leftover wallpaper, tin cans make colorful containers for storing pencils, scissors, and other desk utensils or extra hairbrushes and combs. Use a set to store plastic utensils for outdoor picnics.

- Cans with plastic lids make sturdy containers for nails, screws, hooks, and other hardware.

- Remove the top and bottom of a coffee can and nail to your garage wall to hang brooms and rakes. Fasten the can low enough so that the handle can slide through and rest on the floor.

- Cans are handy in a workshop for sorting paintbrushes, brush end up, as well as holding smaller tools such as putty knives and screwdrivers.

- Store sleeves of cookies or crackers in a covered can to avoid having several mostly empty boxes in the cabinets (especially good for damp environments, such as on the ocean).

before throwing away the envelope. You could also file the invitation in your tickler file.

(see also Storage Solution, page 80)

IRONING BOARD AND IRON

If you use your ironing board regularly, it should be stored in the laundry area or wherever you do your ironing, so you can easily retrieve it or put it away. Or just leave it out if you have the space to do so.

Over-the-door ironing board hangers make it easy to store this cumbersome item without taking up floor space in a closet or room. Some models include a basket to store the iron as well as a bottle of starch or ironing spray.

If you don't often use your ironing board, relegate it to the back of a closet or other out-of-the-way place. When buying a new iron, look for a model with a retractable cord for neater storage.

(see also Laundry Supplies)

I

JACKETS *(see Clothing: Coats and jackets)*

JEANS *(see Clothing: Pants and jeans)*

JEWELRY

Before choosing a method for storing your jewelry, look at what you have. Count rings, earrings, necklaces, bracelets, watches, and pins. That way, you will be able to choose the solution that's best for you.

The traditional way to store jewelry is in a jewelry box or armoire, which I recommend for a large collection and assortment of pieces. Jewelry boxes come in all sizes, shapes, and configurations. While I am attracted to this storage option for the sheer beauty of some of them, I have yet to find a jewelry box that really suits my needs. I prefer individual plush, velvet-lined, compartmentalized jewelry trays that you can stack in drawers.

There are also many options for storing jewelry out in the open, including commercial-type display racks for bracelets, necklaces, and earrings. A jewelry organizer with clear plastic pouches that you can hang from a clothes rod is another inexpensive option for storing all types of jewelry.

(continued)

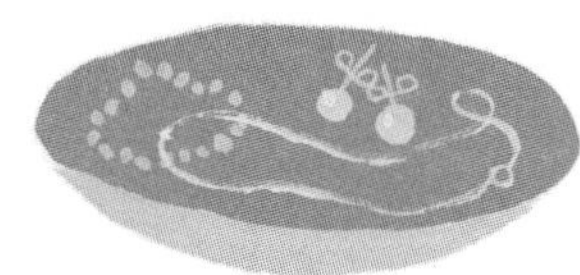

Bowls

Place an attractive bowl on a kitchen countertop or a bedside nightstand, dresser, or hall table to create a temporary home for everyday items such as jewelry, watches, coins, money clips, and wallets.

A decorative bowl placed on a bookshelf can double as a hideaway for small items such as bookmarks, playing cards, and reading glasses. If you place it just above eye level, it can be full of stuff, but nobody will see the clutter — just the bowl.

A large wooden bowl on a coffee table may be the perfect home for television and cable remote controls.

ONE-MINUTE SOLUTION

Keep your jewelry readily accessible by organizing it on the rungs of a multitiered pants hanger. Hang earrings and slide rings over the top rungs. Use lower rungs for bracelets and necklaces. Hang it at the end of your clothes rod, on a wall above your dresser, or the back of your closet door.

Jewelry *(continued)*

To keep infrequently worn silver jewelry from tarnishing, store in a tarnish-preventing bag or wrap it in acid-free tissue and store in a ziplock bag.

One way to safeguard valuable jewelry is to leave a jewelry box in plain sight with pieces of costume jewelry in it. Hang valuables in a bag hidden under an article of clothing or at the bottom of an open box of tissues or other box in your medicine cabinet or under the sink.

(see also Earrings; Necklaces; Rings)

JIGSAW PUZZLES *(see Games/Puzzles)*

KEEPSAKES *(see Knickknacks; Memorabilia)*

KEYS

Wherever you decide to put your keys — on a hook by the door, in a drawer, in the outside pocket of your purse, in a bowl on a table in the entryway, or on your dresser — make it a habit never to just set them down anywhere. Take a few extra moments to put them where they belong and you will never again waste time looking for your keys.

(see also Storage Solutions, pages 131, 142)

KITCHEN APPLIANCES, SMALL

How often do you use your bread maker? Food processor? Coffeemaker? If your answer is every day or at least twice a week, store it on the countertop. If not, store it in a cabinet or with other seasonal or infrequently used items.

glass jars

- Nail metal lids in a row under a cabinet or shelf and screw in the jars for storing dry goods such as beans, popcorn, and rice in the kitchen or hardware in the basement or garage.

- Use baby food or other small jars to store little things like buttons and birthday candles on a shelf or in a drawer.

- Keep one for all the random pieces to things that you find around the house (springs, screws, game or puzzle pieces) so you know where to look when you determine what they belong to.

- Decorate the lids of small jars and use them to hold dried herbs and mixed seasonings.

- A vintage mason jar makes an attractive holder for tea bags, cocoa, sugar, and other kitchen supplies — just make sure it is thoroughly sterilized before use and that the seal is good and tight.

KNICKKNACKS

It might be an assortment of shot glasses from your travels or a collection of porcelain figurines or a bunch of salt and pepper shakers. Whenever possible, display the entire collection in one place to maximize visual appeal.

If space is limited, consider storing a percentage of items and rotating the display periodically rather than having multiple displays, which tend to make a room look cluttered.

KNIVES

If you like to keep your food preparation knives handy, a knife block on the counter is one option. If counter space is limited, consider mounting a magnetic knife bar on the wall or the side of a cabinet, or store them in a wooden knife tray in a drawer.

L

LADDERS

Hang on a garage wall or along rafters to keep the floor clear.

LAUNDRY, CLEAN

Assign a labeled laundry basket to each family member and keep them in the laundry room for carrying clean laundry back to bedrooms. Conserve space if needed by stacking baskets awaiting pickup, alternating each one in a crisscross pattern. Or add a set of freestanding shelves to accommodate the baskets, along with other laundry necessities. Store empty baskets inside each other.

(see also Hangers; Ironing Board and Iron)

LAUNDRY, DIRTY

It makes sense to have a laundry hamper in each family member's room, preferably one with a removable liner or a type that makes it easy to carry dirty clothing to the laundry room. In the laundry room, sort dirty laundry into a three-bin laundry sorter on wheels; label each bin for WHITES (HOT), LIGHTS (WARM), and DARKS (COLD). Hang a small-mesh bag from the sorter for storing items that require a delicate

(continued)

“If I acquire as much as a stone it owns me because I will have to dust it.

HENRY DAVID THOREAU

L

ONE-MINUTE SOLUTION

To minimize wrinkles and piles of clean laundry, fold each load as it comes out of the dryer. Keep the tops of your washer and dryer clear so you have a place to fold. Keep hangers handy.

wash cycle or hand washing. Store the laundry sorter in the laundry room or wheel it to the laundry room from a bedroom closet.

LAUNDRY SUPPLIES

Store all laundry supplies near the washer and dryer. An inexpensive solution is a rolling cart that is specially designed to fit between a washer and dryer.

Another simple solution is a shelf that's specifically designed to attach to the top of a washer. Or you can install shelving or cabinets to organize and store laundry detergent, bleach, fabric softener, iron, and other items.
(see also Ironing Board and Iron)

LAWSUIT PAPERS

Store in a bank safe-deposit box or locked filing cabinet.

LEATHER ITEMS

Store leather shoes, boots, coats, and other items in a dark, airy, cool, dry place that is not too cold or too hot. Direct sunlight will dry leather, as will wind, heat, and dust. To keep leather oils from dissipating and prevent damage while in storage, clean and treat leather with conditioning oil before you store it.

Hang leather coats on extra-wide or padded hangers and stuff the sleeves with tissue paper to help preserve the shape and ward off moisture. Do not cover leather with plastic or store it in a plastic bin. Cover with a cotton sheet or store in a fabric garment bag.

Storage Solution

Hooks

- Add hooks near your entryway to hang keys, coats, backpacks, hats, umbrellas, and more.
- Put hooks behind a bedroom or closet door to hang dry cleaning and laundry bags, pajamas, robe, and clothing that will be worn again soon.
- In the bathroom, add hooks for wet towels, hair dryers, and more.
- Under the kitchen sink, affix a hook or rod inside the cabinet door to hang dish towels or to keep a set of dishwashing gloves handy.
- If you have a door from the garage directly into the house, a series of hooks can be useful for wet jackets, dog-walking supplies, umbrellas, and reusable grocery store totes.

In addition to individual hooks, you can find peg bar and accordion-style hat racks. Over-the-door racks are a simple, space-saving solution that won't mar walls.

Another quick and easy, no-tools solution: Shop for hooks with removable adhesive strips that can be taken down without damaging the wall. You'll find them in all different sizes and colors wherever hardware is sold.

Another way to use hooks is to buy an attractive coat rack (antique stores are a good place to find them). In addition to the usual coats, one near the main entryway can hold handbags, backpacks, umbrellas, and all your canvas shopping totes. If you have a doggy household, designate a coat rack for leashes, dog coats, a supply of pooper-scooper bags, and a couple of towels for wet, muddy feet.

Put one in the guest bedroom with some hangers so guests can use it if you have the closet full of your own belongings. Put one in your own bedroom (or bathroom, if there's room) to hold your pajamas and bathrobe, your favorite sweatshirt, and any clothes you plan to wear again soon.

You can also organize garden tools on an old coat rack. Hang trowels and other digging implements from loops in the handles; lean long-handled tools against the pegs, and use a sturdy canvas tote to hold clippers.

L

LEGAL-SIZED DOCUMENTS

Because most of the paper we file is letter sized, legal-sized documents can present a challenge. If you have a considerable number of legal-sized documents, you might want to designate a filing cabinet drawer for them. Some drawers come equipped with hanging file frames that can be set up to accommodate either letter- or legal-sized documents. You can also buy rails to fit into existing drawers.

But if you only have a handful of legal-sized documents, a simpler solution might be to store them in a legal-sized accordion file or three-ring binder with labeled divider tabs to separate contents by transaction or case. Of course, you can always fold legal documents to fit into a letter-sized file (yes, it's okay!). Fold some from the bottom, some from the top, and some in the middle to reduce bulk.

(see Storage Solutions, pages 15, 160, 188)

LIGHTBULBS

Gather and store all household lightbulbs in one central place, such as a linen or hall closet. Store in a labeled bin or paper bag on a shelf, not on the floor, where a heavy object could fall and break the bulbs. Alternatively, stash bulbs in strategic locations throughout your home, such as a linen closet, bathroom, and upstairs chest of drawers, for ready access when needed.

LINENS

The linen closet, if you have one, is the obvious choice for storing linens. But it's actually more efficient to store linens in the rooms in which they are used. Towels can be stored in bathrooms, folded and stacked by size on shelves or rolled in a large basket. Storing towels in the laundry room is another option that makes sense.

Bedding can be kept on shelves in a bedroom closet, under a bed, or in a chest of drawers or trunk. If you do store all your linens in a linen closet, labeling shelves will help to keep the closet organized, as will using shelf dividers.

L

ONE-MINUTE SOLUTION

Store sheets as a "grab-and-go" set by inserting the folded fitted sheet and pillowcases in the last fold of the flat sheet. Or store the folded sheets and pillowcases inside a matching pillow case.

Store off-season linens, comforters, blankets, and pillows in sealed plastic bags, containers, or trunks with cedar chips or blocks. Replace or rejuvenate with cedar oil every few months. Or store linens with moth-repellent sachets made of dried lemon peels or dried lavender and cedar chips. Wash all out-of-season linens before storing.

(see also Quilts/Comforters/Blankets; Sheets; Table Linens; Towels; Storage Solutions, pages 60, 75)

LIQUOR

The best place to store liquor depends on how often you drink it. If you drink or serve it regularly or use it for cooking, keep liquor handy in a kitchen cabinet, ideally with or near cocktail glasses. If you don't want or need regular access to liquor, you may want to store it on a high shelf or in the back of a cabinet. Some people like to store liquors such as tequila and vodka in the freezer for a smoother shot.

If there's any chance of accidental ingestion or abuse by an underage child, consider locking up your liquor. You can buy a special liquor cabinet with a lock, lock it in a home safe, or use a lock on a cabinet door or trunk.

Wherever you store liquor, keep bottles tightly capped. Store away from direct sunlight and heat sources and avoid exposure to extreme changes in temperature. Alcohol, unlike wine or beer, will still be good a decade or more after opening, with the exception of cream-based liqueurs, which should be refrigerated to prolong shelf life.

(see also Wine)

L

LIVING WILL

Store the original at home in a fire- and burglar-resistant safe. Give copies to a close family member and to your doctor.

(see also Storage Solutions, pages 32, 188)

LOCAL AREA INFORMATION

Make your own visitors guide. Gather local maps, including a map of your neighborhood, and put them in a three-ring binder along with event flyers, take-out menus, and brochures for points of interest such as museums, theaters, parks, golf courses, bowling alleys, and scenic vistas. Use divider tabs to organize information for easy reference.

You also could include a list of movie theaters, favorite restaurants, and shopping destinations with addresses and phone numbers, and anything else that might be a handy resource for your family and guests. Store the guide with the phone directory, in your communications center, home office, guest room, or with other reference books.

(see also Storage Solution, page 168)

LUGGAGE *(see Suitcases)*

M

ONE-MINUTE SOLUTION

Vintage and collectible magazines and comic books should be stored in special protective bags in acid-free boxes designed to resist dust, dirt, and light infiltration. Look for them online or in stores selling scrapbooking or photo-booking supplies.

MAGAZINES

Here's a little-known device for storing magazines, catalogs, comic books, and manuals in binders: It's a specially designed strip of plastic; one side slips inside the magazine to secure it and the other side is hole-punched to fit into any three-ring binder.

My favorite way to store magazines and comic books is vertically in a special magazine file box. You can find these files in every material to match your decor, from acrylic to cloth to leather. Sort magazines by title and then arrange by date.

Magazine file boxes look great on bookshelves. Just one problem: You will soon run out of room if you store every issue of every magazine, won't you? If it's certain articles you want to save, as most people do, tear them out and file them in a binder.

If, for instance, you save decorating magazines, label a three-ring binder HOME DECORATING and divide it into sections for bathroom, bedroom, kitchen, living areas, office, outdoor, and other. File articles and product pages from catalogs in the appropriate sections and you've got a handy reference of great ideas. *(see also Catalogs; Comic Books; Storage Solutions, pages 160, 168)*

MAIL

Set up an inbox with multiple slots to sort incoming mail for various family members. Your inbox might be as simple as a basket on a stand near the primary entryway, a box on a kitchen counter, or a file folder on a desk in your den or office. Make it a goal to regularly empty your inbox: ideally every day, but minimally every week or when the box is full.

M

Open and sort every item: immediately toss outer envelopes, unwanted flyers, and other junk into the trash or recycling bin; shred preapproved credit card offers and anything with an account number or personally identifiable information; file bills to be paid and other papers that you need to keep or respond to; transfer magazines and catalogs to their keeping places.

MAKEUP *(see Cosmetics)*

MANUALS, PRODUCT

One option is to store all of your product manuals in a filing cabinet in file folders. Create a hanging file for each room in which the products reside (including the garage and workshop). Within each room folder, file alphabetically by product name (e.g., television, refrigerator, or power tools) or by manufacturer (e.g., Amana, Craftsman). File the manuals open-end down in the folders, all facing front and in the same direction.

An alternative to filing manuals in a cabinet is to file them in an accordion file. Label sections as described above. Another option is to store product manuals in binders. Put the manuals in heavy-duty

(continued)

Storage Solution

Containers

The right storage container can go a long way toward helping you maintain organization. I always recommend clear plastic storage boxes. Why? Because you can see what's inside without having to open the box. These lidded containers come in lots of different sizes; they're fairly inexpensive and watertight; and they protect contents from dirt, insects, and rodents.

Use lidded containers everywhere in the house for storing a variety of items — craft and hobby items, shoes, scarves, mittens and gloves, purses, holiday decorations, and sports gear. Ideally, you'll use same-size boxes so they stack easily in your storage space.

Label the front of every bin and all four sides so you can turn and rearrange boxes if needed.

Manuals, Product *(continued)*
sheet protectors and place them in a 3-inch (7.6 cm) binder. Use indexed tabs to divide the binder into sections by room and then file manuals alphabetically as described above. Label the front and spine of the binder for easy identification and store on a shelf somewhere. You may need to create several binders.

You might also store manuals in designated places in a room: for example, all kitchen appliances in a kitchen cabinet and drawer or manuals for all household systems such as furnace, hot-water heater, and water softener on a shelf in the garage.

Whatever method you choose, be sure to discard any manuals that go with products you no longer own!
(see also Storage Solution, page 168)

MAPS, DESTINATION TRAVEL

Designate a drawer or create a hanging file for storing travel brochures and maps with labeled files for individual destinations. Or create a PLACES TO GO binder.
(see also Storage Solutions, pages 160, 168)

MAPS, LOCAL

It's not a bad idea to keep at least one good local map in your vehicle. If you have more than one, consider

(continued)

hatboxes and decorative tins

- Sturdy, attractive hatboxes or large decorative tins make neat containers for storing memorabilia and keepsakes.
- They provide a classy way to store gloves, silk scarves, or lingerie.
- Use one to protect evening bags, fancy shoes, and other special-occasion items.
- Tuck one in a corner of a small powder room to hold clean guest towels and an extra roll of toilet tissue.
- Store tea lights and candle tarts in a drawer in an old cookie tin.
- Cookie tins make great holders for ribbons and trim for sewing and for gift wrapping; also for gift tags.
- Use one to organize your manicure and pedicure supplies.

M

Maps *(continued)*
storing them all in the glove box or driver-door compartment. Alternatively, file local/regional/state maps in your house with local interest books (if you have any) or wherever you store other local reference materials, such as the phone book.
(see also Local Area Information)

MARRIAGE CERTIFICATES

Store in a fire- and burglar-resistant safe or in a bank safe-deposit box. Make a copy for the executor of your estate.

MATERIAL *(see Fabric)*

MEDICAL RECORDS

Your patient history is on file with your physician, but you may want to store copies of medical records yourself. Set up a hanging file with interior file folders for each family member to keep track of medical professionals and facilities visited as well as records of allergies, blood type, and lab test results.

Store receipts for paid bills, including prescriptions, with your current-year tax records. Staple bills to the corresponding Explanation of Benefits (EOB) statements.
(see also Tax Records; X-rays; Storage Solutions, pages 160, 168)

Clutter is physical proof of your abundance. Be generous and donate the stuff that's just taking up valuable space in your home. **Someone, somewhere could really use it.**

M

MEDICATIONS

The Community Medical Foundation for Patient Safety recommends the following measures:

» Every six months or when you add new medications to your medicine cabinet, dispose of all expired medicines and those that you are not using, even if they are not expired. Always keep medications, vitamins, and supplements in original containers.

» Keep only medicines and first-aid items in your medicine cabinet.

» Store medications in a cool, dry place, away from sunlight.

» Do not store medications in the bathroom if ventilation is poor and it is too damp.

» Use shelves to separate medicines for different family members.

» Keep all medications (including pill organizers or boxes) beyond the reach of children and use a child-safety lock on the medicine cabinet.

» Keep prescription information sheets close to your medications.

MEMBERSHIP CARDS *(see Frequent Flyer Cards)*

Label everything – from shelves in your medicine cabinet, pantry and linen closet to children's dresser drawers, bins, and baskets. If a label won't stick to an item such as a basket, attach a metal ring label or make a label using a sturdy paper tag and ribbon or twine.

M

MEMORABILIA

Store keepsakes and mementos in a special box. When the box gets full, pare down to just those things that are still meaningful to you. To preserve items longer, especially photos and paper, consider storing memorabilia in an archival media box.

(see also Artwork, Children's; Knickknacks; Trophies and Awards; Storage Solution, page 153)

Storage Solution

File folders

One of the simplest ways to store papers is to purchase a ready-made filing system for home or business. Why? Because if you have to make a file, you'll probably just put the paper into a "to-be-filed" pile.

When creating file labels, think of the first word that would pop into your head if you were looking for that item or category of items.

Keep hanging files and interior folders handy for those files that you still need to make.

You're more likely to use an organizing product if you love it. Instead of settling for plain manila, look for colored or patterned file folders that suit your personal style or match your decor to store frequently accessed papers.

Avoid stuffing folders too full. Use staplers rather than paper clips to keep related papers together and store flat rather than folded (except for legal-size documents).

File current project folders or active ones such as Bills to Pay and Receipts to Enter in vertical standing files or in stacking desk trays or wall baskets labeled the same way you would label hanging folders. At the end of each year, go through your files to weed out any papers you no longer need to store.

(see also Legal-Sized Documents; Papers; Storage Solutions, pages 15, 80, 196)

M

MENUS, TAKEOUT

Hang menus you refer to often on the refrigerator with a magnetic clip. Or store in a drawer or folder near the phone. You might even program numbers for your favorite restaurants into your telephone.
(see also Local Area Information; Storage Solution, page 168)

MILITARY DISCHARGE PAPERS

Store in a bank safe-deposit box.

MITTENS AND GLOVES *(see Gloves and Mittens)*

MORTGAGE OR HOME LOAN PAPERS

Create a separate file folder for each property owned. Store in a locked file cabinet or bank safe-deposit box along with other real estate records, such as insurance information, tax notices, and receipts for home improvements. Keep the notice of mortgage payoff indefinitely.
(see also Storage Solution, page 32)

MRIs *(see X-rays)*

MULTIMEDIA MATERIALS *(see CDs and DVDs; Videotapes)*

MUSIC BOOKS AND SHEET MUSIC

Store a small collection of sheet music and books in a file box with dividers for various types of music. If portability is required, opt for an accordion-style file or binder with dividers and sheet protectors or use a large, sturdy gift bag or a boutique shopping bag.

I recommend shelving larger collections. Arrange music books with a title on the binding as you would shelve books. Label the front of shelves and use bookends to divide categories. Store thinner books (and sheet music) in magazine files, labeled and organized by genre or composer.

A filing cabinet is often the best solution for an extensive collection of sheet music. Set up hanging folders for each category and then use interior folders for subcategories. Box-bottom folders will also accommodate slim books of music. Another option is to design and build cabinets or shelving with narrow cubbies.

M

ONE-MINUTE SOLUTION

Digitize your music collection. Copy music from audio CDs and MP3 files using Windows Media Player or Apple iTunes. You can then copy songs to a portable digital device or create custom mix CDs.

MUSICAL INSTRUMENTS

Never store a musical instrument in direct sunlight or near a heat source. Leaving an instrument in a car on a hot, sunny day can result in damage. Protect from extreme dryness (low-humidity environments).

Do not allow a woodwind instrument to get wet or the pads that cover the holes will absorb water and no longer cover the holes correctly. Store sections separately in its case. Store extra reeds, swabs, and other cleaning supplies in your instrument case or a pencil case.

N

NECKLACES

It's best to hang fine chain necklaces to keep them from tangling — use a wooden tie rack or freestanding jewelry rack.

Another option is to store them in ice cube trays or egg cartons, one chain per section.

You can also use extra wall space to display jewelry on a canvas-covered artist frame (painted or unpainted) or felted board; use U-shaped pins to attach necklaces and earrings to it.

(see also Jewelry)

NECKTIES *(see Belts and Neckties)*

NEGATIVES AND SLIDES

Keep negatives clean and protect them from light, heat, and humidity. If necessary, clean dust and fingerprints from negatives before storing. Do not store negatives or slides in drawers or closets where you keep clothing or fabric, as these materials attract insects that may decide to feed on them.

Store negatives in metal drawers or file boxes and keep away from sunlight and heat sources, such as radiators, warm-air registers, chimneys, and heat ducts.

If storing at room temperature (recommended for short-term storage only), maintain a relative humidity lower than 60 percent to prevent mold and fungus. Store in archival-quality plastic envelopes or sleeves or paper envelopes. To preserve quality and extend life, store negatives in the freezer in special, moisture-proof envelopes, also known as vapor-seal envelopes, to protect from humidity. Pack each envelope lightly, not tight, and remove excess air. Avoid stacking to prevent pressure on stored negatives.

NEWSPAPERS

Why do you save newspapers? They can be a fire hazard. But maybe you *do* want to start a fire with them! In that case, store a small pile of newspapers in a dry place near your fireplace, where they are handy when you need them.

If it's only a few articles you want to save, that's different! Go ahead and clip those items and, if you are collecting clippings on a particular subject, set up a three-ring binder with prepunched sheet protectors. Otherwise, recycle those newspapers, even if you have not read them. By tomorrow, it will all be old news.
(see also Storage Solution, page 168)

N

Storage Solution

Binders

Binder storage is a good alternative to file folders for reference materials and other information you frequently need to look up, such as school schedules. Binders are also an excellent tool for storing information that needs to be portable, such as medical records for an ongoing condition. And you can create binders for recipes to try or home decorating ideas torn from the pages of your favorite magazines (rather than storing the magazines).

Many families find it helpful to create a handy reference guide for sports schedules, school calendars, PTA/PTO information, and emergency contact information, as well as contact information for schools and service providers such as housekeeper, babysitter, travel agent, airport shuttle, and delivery and repair people. Your family notebook also may include take-out menus, local retailer coupons, and a calendar with birthday/anniversary reminders.

All you need is a binder, a set of three-hole-punched, top-loading sheet protectors, and divider tabs.

Tip: Be sure that the plastic sheets do not overlap the divider tabs. If you don't want to make your own, shop for ready-made family organizer binders.

(see also Magazines)

N

ONE-MINUTE SOLUTION

A large collection of books, DVDs, CDs, wines, or other items can be cataloged quickly and easily with a handheld bar-code scanner. Accompanying software automatically fills in details about each item from an extensive Internet database. Your personal database can include additional information, such as location and notes.

NOTES

Keep an office message pad (with carbon-copy sheets) near the main home phone and attach a pen to it. Train yourself and your family members to date and record all voice-mail and live-caller messages here. If you misplace the original message, you can refer back to the carbon-copy records.

You can also use this system to write notes to your family such as "Went grocery shopping. Be back at 5." Or record all voicemail messages and notes in a journal or lined notebook.

(continued)

tote bags

- Use small ones to sort and store a large stash of yarn.
- Keep one by the door to collect things such as library books that need to be returned.
- Hang a couple on pegs in the utility room to store specialized clothing (biking and horseback riding gear, ski wear, work clothing or uniforms) off the floor and ready to go.
- A tote in the laundry room works well for keeping clothes that need pretreatment separated from the regular laundry.
- A large one can hold all your skates (ice or roller) and helmets so you can grab everything at once and head out the door to the rink or the park.
- Use one to hold all those power adapters and random cords that pile up.
- Hang several in a bedroom or hall closet to hold shoes, belts, winter accessories, and other items for easy access.
- Small ones could hang on a hook in a closet to hold pet supplies, umbrellas, flashlights, etc., or use one for those darn TV remotes.
- Keep a tote in your car or by the door with sunscreen, bug spray, and hand wipes to grab on your way to a picnic or other outdoor event.

Notes *(continued)*

If you have a tendency to write bits and pieces of information on sticky notes or notepaper, try this: Jot it all down in a small, colorful spiral notebook that you carry everywhere. Train yourself to write notes only in your notebook. If the notebook is not nearby, you'll have to go get it.

Date each page and keep all the information on those pages or transfer some or all information to your address book, day planner, or other storage place. If you need to reference your notes, you'll know where to find them.

If you spend most of your time in front of the computer, use the Notes and Tasks features in Microsoft Outlook or create a document for notes. When you're on the go, type notes into your PDA or cell phone datebook (mine is under Tools). Select a date and type in appointments, reminders, and notes for that date.

A less tedious option is to call home and leave a message on your voice mail or use one of several online services that will transcribe a voice message into an e-mail to yourself.

O

ODDS AND ENDS

Designate a catchall container — a small dish, basket, or junk drawer — to collect items that have yet to find a home or need temporary living quarters, such as a button that needs to be sewn back on a shirt or a part that goes to something but you can't remember what. Periodically sort through and make decisions about what to keep and what to toss.

(see also Baskets; Storage Solutions, pages 16, 131)

OFFICE/SCHOOL SUPPLIES

Set up a mini-warehouse where you can "shop" for paper clips, rubber bands, staples, notepads, pens, pencils, markers, erasers, and other office/school supplies. Gather them all in one place so you can see what you have and how much room you need.

Then designate a storage location. It could be a kitchen or desk drawer, a cabinet shelf, a lidded box in the linen or hall closet, or a mobile storage unit.

Hint: Hang a reorder list for noting items that are out of stock or in low supply.

(see also Storage Solutions, pages 40, 153)

ORNAMENTS *(see Decorations, Seasonal)*

Overhead storage

Store boxes and other bulky items off the floor and out of the way by turning unused ceiling space into valuable storage space with an overhead organizer in the garage, attic, or basement. You can also install one in a closet. These units keep your belongings safe and dry and help avoid damage caused by insects or rodents.

If you have built-in cabinets, use the tops to store infrequently used items. Hang whatever you can from walls, rafters, or ceilings, especially seasonal items such as bicycles and snow tires. Hang ladders too.

In a garage, make your main goal to store things off the floor so you have more room to park vehicles and still move around.

tv armoire

If you've upgraded your home entertainment center with a flat-screen television, you might be wondering what to do with your old armoire. Here are four ways to convert it into a fabulous new storage solution.

- Remove shelves and drawers, install a rod, and use it as a coat closet or place to store off-season clothing.

- Add shelves to create a linen closet or utility closet in a hallway or workshop.

- Remove doors, add shelves, and make it a bookcase or display case.

- Adjust the main shelf to desk height, remove any lower drawers, and add some upper shelves and/or cubbyholes, and you've got a hideaway office for a living room corner or kid's room.

ONE-MINUTE SOLUTION

Label paint cans with the room or items that it was used on such as FRONT HALL or DOWNSTAIRS BATH. You might even dab a spot of paint on the lid.

P

PAINT

When storing paint, carefully clean the groove around the top of the can. Lay a piece of plastic wrap about an inch larger than the top of the can before putting the lid on to ensure an airtight seal. Be careful not to damage the lid. Place a block of wood over the lid and tap it with a hammer.

Store paint cans upside down on a shelf. Do not store directly on a concrete floor, as moisture may cause cans to rust. Avoid extremes in temperature.

Freezing and thawing latex paint will cause it to separate and spoil; subjecting oil-based paint to extreme heat is a fire hazard.

Paint does have a shelf life. However, if you open a can and mix it well and it looks good, it probably is good. Discard old paint and empty paint cans as household hazardous waste.

PAJAMAS *(see Clothing: Pajamas)*

PANTRY ITEMS

Store canned and packaged foods in a cool (below 70°F/21°C), dry area, away from light. Avoid storing these foods in cabinets near the oven, on shelves near the ceiling, or near a radiator or baseboard heater.

Maximize storage space with freestanding shelves, under-shelf baskets, stepped organizers, two-tiered turntables, and stacking containers to keep items such as chips, dried fruit, nuts, and sugars fresh and to corral seasoning packets, tea bags, and other small items. Label the container fronts. Shelves also may be labeled.

Sliding baskets make it easy to access items at the back of a cabinet. If you need extra storage space in a pantry, consider installing a rack on the back of the door for easy access to frequently used items such as olive oil, peanut butter, honey, salt boxes, and bread crumbs.

Stay organized by using these tips:

» Designate shelves or sections of shelves for certain categories of foods such as grains (pastas and rices), canned meat and fish, vegetables, fruit, beans, baking supplies, and snack foods.
» Arrange cans, bottles, and boxes on shelves with the labels facing out.
» Store older items at the front of your food cabinets and newer items at the back.
» Consider marking the item farthest back with a colored sticky flag to let you know it's the last of its kind.

(see also Storage Solutions, pages 60, 224)

PANTS *(see Clothing: Pants and jeans)*

PANTY HOSE *(see Clothing: Socks and panty hose)*

Q. Where should you store items you never use?*

a. Basement

b. Attic

c. Garage

d. Shed

e. Off-site storage

** Sorry, that was a trick question. If you have no need for something, why are you storing it?*

“

. . . a man’s life does not consist in the abundance of his possessions.

LUKE 12:15

PAPERS

What? You've got piles of paper in your home? I'd be surprised if you didn't! Here's a great way to get it all sorted out and organized so you can store it away — and find it again if you need it.

Quickly (and I mean quickly!) sort all the paper piles into three categories: To Do, To File, and To Toss. Your To Do pile might include bills to pay, forms to fill out, a card or letter to respond to, newsletters and magazines to read, directions to an upcoming party, or event tickets. Your To File pile will include tax records, insurance policies, manuals, and receipts.

Before putting items into this pile, however, ask yourself: Is this something I will need to look at again? Do I need to save it for tax or legal purposes? Is this information difficult to retrieve if I should need it someday?

If the answer to all three questions is no, toss it. Also trash expired coupons, outdated flyers, and old shopping lists and notes. Do be sure to shred any paper with your Social Security number or account numbers before trashing.

After this initial sort, store the To Do papers in a tickler file or folders labeled for action categories such as To Pay, To Call, and To Read. Pull out the most

(continued)

ice cube trays

- Fill each cube with a fine chain necklace or pairs of earrings and stack them in a drawer.
- Use in the sewing room to separate safety pins, buttons, hooks and eyes, snaps, and so on.
- Ice cube trays can also be used for storing paper clips, and other small items in a desk drawer.

important documents, such as tax records, and file them immediately. Keep current documents in your home office workspace; store archival documents such as tax records in a more out-of-the-way location. Store important legal and financial documents in a fire- and burglar-resistant safe or bank safe-deposit box.

Avoid storing paper in cardboard boxes in the attic, basement, garage, or off-site unit. Flooding may destroy them, and insects and rodents are always on the lookout for a nice paper snack or bedding material.
(see also Storage Solutions, pages 15, 32, 80, 160, 188, 196)

PARTY DECORATIONS

Pack a small amount of decorations in a labeled container (clear plastic boxes with lids are perfect). A larger collection of decorations may require several containers, organized and labeled by theme or type of party such as VALENTINE'S DAY or OVER THE HILL birthday. Choose containers large enough to hold everything, including tablecloths, serving platters, napkins, paper plates, candles, and so on. Store containers on the upper shelf of a kitchen cabinet or closet, or in your garage, basement, or attic.
(see also Decorations, Seasonal)

P

ONE-MINUTE SOLUTION

Leave a copy of your passport data page with family or friends when traveling. Make a note of your passport number and expiration date and keep it separate from your passport. This information will facilitate replacement in the event that your passport is lost or stolen.

PASSPORTS

Store at home in a fire- and burglar-resistant safe. You could store passports in a bank safe-deposit box, but keep in mind that if you ever need immediate access to your passport during non-banking hours, you will not be able to obtain it.

Avoid excessive bending and keep away from water, solvents, and other liquids. Shred outdated passports.

PASSWORDS, ELECTRONIC

Storing passwords in a file — any file — on your computer is not recommended because computer files are not secure. Convenient as it is, having your computer remember or store user names and passwords associated with various accounts could be risky. If an unscrupulous individual gains physical access to your computer, it's a bit like leaving the key to the house under the front-door mat.

Using a single password to log into all of your accounts is equally risky, especially for your financial and e-mail accounts. If that password becomes known through a breach of security at one site, the hacker may attempt to gain access to other sites where your personal and financial information are exposed.

There are a number of online password safes and password manager programs available, some free of charge. Some are desktop applications that are stored on your hard drive and some of these allow you to "carry" passwords and other data with you on your PDA or a USB flash drive, giving you portable access. Others store your information online, in which case you need an Internet connection to access your passwords. Before you choose one of these options, do the

(continued)

P

Storage Solution

Scanner

Scanners allow you to convert paper documents, such as bank and investment statements, to electronic files that you can organize and store on your computer. Scanned papers can be shredded after you back up the files.

There are several types of scanners available, including some designed specifically for scanning business cards or receipts. Do some research, including reading online forums for user reviews, to determine which type of scanner is best for your needs.

The best (albeit priciest) in my book is a document scanner. Much faster than flatbed scanners (8–10 pages per minute), document scanners let you load multiple pages into the feeder. They scan double-sided paper and include software that allows you categorize, label, find, and retrieve documents by searching for any word in the document.

(see also Storage Solution, page 196)

research to make sure you understand exactly how your passwords are stored.

The safest place to store passwords is in your head. But how is that possible? you ask. Simple. Create a personal password template. For example, you might combine the first and last three letters of an account or Web site name with numbers that represent the birthday of your spouse or firstborn child. Thus, if you are creating a password for online banking at Bank of America and your spouse was born on May 24, your password might be Ban524icA. Using upper- and lowercase letters makes your password stronger.

Another option is to have one base password with a combination of six letters and numbers and then add on the first and last letters of the account or Web site name. If you create passwords by applying the same pattern to all, you will be able to remember an unlimited number of passwords for use with Web-based e-mail, online banking, credit card transactions, and all other Web sites where personal information is stored.

If you'd like, you can then choose a single, simple password for use with all nonsecured Web sites. Even then, never use an obvious password such as your birth date, mother's maiden name, or the last four digits of your Social Security number. And don't use the base password you use for secure sites.

You may opt to store passwords in a paper-based address directory under the first letter of the account or Web site name or write them in a list. Although a paper list cannot be hacked, you still need to keep it safe from physical theft. One way to do that is always to add an extra letter or number or two to the beginning and end of every password in your paper directory. For security, store your password list in a fire- and burglar-resistant safe. And let another family member know where to find it in the event that you are unable to tell him or her.

If you're not overly concerned about theft but want to keep your list handy while still playing it safe, you could always tape a file folder under your desk and then store your password directory there. Or file it in a folder with a bland or unappealing label such as MAPS or STOMACH SURGERY.

PENSION PLAN DOCUMENTS

Store in a locked filing cabinet or bank safe-deposit box.

ONE-MINUTE SOLUTION

Create a home for pet toys and teach your pets where to find them. If you can also get them to put their toys away, more power to you!

P

PET FOOD

Store dry pet food in a tightly sealed container to keep freshness in, pesky rodents and insects out. A large plastic food container might be just right for storing pet food or treats in a pantry or near food bowls. An empty, lidded cat litter bucket can be recycled to hold the contents of a small bag of dog or cat food. A small metal trash can serves the purpose for larger bags. It's a good idea to label containers, especially recycled containers.

tackle boxes

- Tackle boxes are a neat way to organize and store tools and other hardware in the garage or you can use one as a traveling house repair kit. The sections are perfect for separating screws, picture hangers, and nails by size. A hammer and screwdrivers fit easily in the bottom.

- Store batteries and electronic parts in the top trays; stash battery chargers, extra headphones, and other electronic equipment in the larger compartment.

- They offer a great way to sort and store arts and crafts supplies for beading, jewelry-making, sewing, watercolors — anything you can think of!

- Turn one into a traveling Barbie suitcase! The hook and bait sections hold those tiny high heels and other accessories, while the other compartments keep outfits organized. Barbie herself fits in the bottom with any larger items.

- Turn a small one into a first-aid kit for car or camping.

PET PARAPHERNALIA

Gather and sort all the pet stuff into categories such as grooming tools and products, food and bowls, toys, sweaters and raincoats, leashes and collars, and waste disposal items.

Store food and bowls near your pet feeding area; cat litter and litter disposal tools near the litter box. If you have multiple cats and therefore multiple boxes, having a container of litter and a scooper by each box makes it much quicker and easier to clean them out.

Hang leashes, harnesses, and waste-disposal bags near the door. Store other items in baskets or storage containers on shelves.

Create a folder for each pet with its medical history, vaccination records, rabies certificates, and license documents. File with other family records.

PHOTOGRAPHS

If you only have digital images, you may prefer to store them on your computer and use a program to organize them into albums that you can share with others, and then print only selected photos. You also can display digital images in portable digital frames and albums. You might also consider creating a unique slide show or screensaver for your computer using stored photos or scanned memorabilia.

Store prints in the main area of your home, away from light, heat, and humidity. Store negatives in a safe-deposit box in archival envelopes labeled by date. To preserve photographs longer, use archival-quality photo boxes or photo album pages.

Organize a backlog of photographs by sorting them into three to five broad categories. Categories might be friends, family, children, grandchildren, places you've lived, places you've visited. Or you can categorize by events (graduations) or by time frames (college days) or by family members. As you sort, toss photos into labeled boxes or paper bags.

Next, starting with one box or bag, sort photographs into subcategories. For example, if your main category is VACATIONS, sort photographs into separate vacations you've taken. A labeled shoe box works well for organizing; use durable sticky tabs to create subcategory labels. I use the kind of photo sorter that scrapbookers use. It's a big lidded box with a dozen smaller, removable boxes that can be labeled.

As you sort photographs, throw away ones that didn't come out right or are similar to better

(continued)

bungee cords

Screw hooks into a wall and attach bungee cords to either end so that the bungee cords are drawn tight to the wall. Measure the cords first so you know how far apart to space the hooks. They need to be snug enough to hold items in place. Use the bungee cords to:

- Transform the interior walls or inside door of a hall closet into a storage space for mittens, gloves, hats and scarves.
- Line a mudroom wall with several rows of bungee cords and use them to keep the floor clear of shoes.
- Store shoes or purses on the back of a bedroom closet door.
- String cords in the garage to secure tennis racquets, hockey and lacrosse sticks, baseball bats, and other tall sports gear.
- Install hooks in your laundry room or bathroom and attach bungee cords to serve as a clothesline for hanging drip-dry items when you need to. Store the bungee cord and clothespins in a bag from one hook when not in use.

Storage Solution

Computer

Using your computer to store and manage contacts, to-do lists, documents, personal information such as genealogies, photographs, receipts, and data is one way to reduce paper. Don't store all of your important documents on your computer desktop, though: That's like leaving all your papers out on your desk, which makes it difficult to find anything.

Instead, create folders by subject to store related documents in the same way you would if you were filing the physical pieces of paper in a filing cabinet. Similarly, instead of saving all incoming e-mails in your inbox, save them to your subject folders.

Do be sure to perform frequent backups of your hard drive. When backing up to disks was the only option, I found it too time consuming. Backing up to an external hard drive backup is faster and easier, but if your home or office is burglarized and your computer

is stolen, chances are the thief will take the external hard drive, too.

Thumb-drive backup is a good option for backing up your laptop while away from home, but I prefer online backup because it's automatic, which means one less thing I have to remember. For about $50 a year, all your documents are backed up within minutes of creating or modifying them.

(see also Addresses; Business Cards; Passwords, Electronic; Storage Solution, page 188)

P

ONE-MINUTE SOLUTION

Don't keep adding new photographs to piles of old ones. Start a photo album with your most recent photographs. Continue to add to it, and all your photographs from today forward will be organized.

Photographs *(continued)*

photographs. Throw out duplicates or, if you can't bring yourself to do that, put them into a separate box labeled DUPLICATES and share with family members.

If you never get any further than this step, at least all your photographs will be sorted instead of stored in a jumbled mess. Store photo albums on shelves as you would books.

(see also Books; Storage Solution, page 196)

PILLOWS

Store extra pillows in a guest room, on a closet shelf or in a dresser drawer. Keep them dust-free by placing them in their original plastic packaging or wrapped in a dry cleaning bag. But do not store down pillows in plastic; cover with a pillowcase or other breathable fabric instead.

(see also Linens)

POCKET PARAPHERNALIA

You know what I mean . . . keys, coins, wallet, cell phone, receipts, gum, mints, whatever. Keep a pretty bowl or basket on your dresser or near the front entryway for those items that you will load back into your pockets tomorrow.

Here's a suggestion: Get in the habit of putting all loose change in a piggybank to save for a rainy day or give to your favorite charity. A dollar in change each day adds up to $365 in a year.

POT LIDS

You could store every lid on top of the pot it belongs to, but that would take up too much room. You could just toss them all into a cabinet, but that's not very organized. What you need are pot lid organizers. They come in a variety of sizes and styles from inexpensive, freestanding racks to pricier (but worth every penny) pullout racks. A dish-drying rack will also do the trick.

Storage Solution

Turntables (lazy Susans)

Put turntables in corner cabinets to make it easy to access everything. They come in all different sizes. I use large turntables in our bathroom linen closet to store extra supplies of toiletries on one shelf and first-aid supplies on another.

You can use turntables in your refrigerator, too, to prevent leftovers from getting lost and forgotten. Smaller, two-tiered turntables are good for storing medicine bottles, spice jars, or canned goods in cabinets or on pantry shelves.

POTS AND PANS

Make it easy to retrieve and put away the ones you use most frequently — store them in the cabinet closest to the stove or hang them overhead from a pot rack.

Stack pots and pans to save space. Place a layer of paper toweling or a terry washcloth between nonstick pans to prevent scratching. Consider installing roll-out drawers for pots and pans. Create extra storage space in a cabinet by removing roasting pans, lobster pots, and other large, infrequently used pots and pans to a shelf in the garage or up high in a coat closet.
(see also Storage Solution, page 60)

POWER-OF-ATTORNEY PAPERS

Store a copy in a fire- and burglar-resistant safe or bank safe-deposit box. Also give a copy to a close family member. Have your attorney keep the original. Shred papers that have been revised.

PRESCRIPTIONS *(see Medications)*

PROPERTY TAX STATEMENTS

Store with current-year tax records in a filing cabinet.

P

PURSES

My favorite purse storage solutions are organizers that hang on the wall or on the back of a closet or bedroom door. This type of display makes it quick and easy to see what you have and to put purses away. You can also find special purse organizers that hang from a clothes rod or you can use a hanging sweater shelf organizer.

The only downside to leaving all of your purses on display is that the ones you don't use often collect dust. Store infrequently used purses in clear plastic bins that you can stack and store on a shelf.

You also might use clear plastic zippered bags like the ones that are used to package new linens. Underbed storage containers are a good spot for evening bags, as well as fancy hosiery and lingerie that don't get used much.

PUZZLES *(see Games/Puzzles)*

QUILTS/COMFORTERS/BLANKETS

Fold and store extra quilts, comforters (except down), and blankets on shelves or in a trunk in clear plastic zippered bags or other storage bags to keep them clean and fresh. Another option is to hang more frequently used blankets on a towel rod on the back of a bedroom door.

Down comforters should not be stored in plastic. Wrap down bedding in a breathable fabric such as a cotton pillowcase. Be sure your comforter is completely dry before storing and store it in a dry place.

One recommended way to store antique quilts is to lay them on an unused bed and cover them with a clean sheet or coverlet. If a quilt must be folded for storage, layer it between two clean white sheets and fold in accordion pleats. Materials such as plastic, cardboard, and wood can damage delicate fabrics, so make sure a quilt is covered and is entirely dry before boxing it.

To display an antique quilt, sew a fabric sleeve along the top and use a sturdy dowel to distribute the weight. Don't hang a quilt for more than six months at a time, and always keep antique fabrics protected from sunlight.

(see also Linens; Storage Solution, page 75)

“

How many things I can do without.

SOCRATES

OUT OF THE BOX
Organizer
Transforming Common Items into Storage Solutions

checkbook boxes

Wrap them in contact paper or heavy gift-wrapping paper for a cheerful look and then put them to use.

- They make great drawer organizers for pens and pencils and other desk doodads.
- Use one as a jewelry box when you are traveling.
- Keep stamps and address labels handy in your bill-paying area.
- Place one or more boxes in a cutlery drawer to organize special utensils such as measuring spoons, cheese spreaders, bottle openers and corkscrews, and paring knives.
- Use several to corral small items in a junk drawer.

R

REAL ESTATE TRANSACTION DOCUMENTS

Store in a locked filing cabinet for as long as you own your home plus 10 years after a change in ownership.
(see also Storage Solution, page 188)

RECEIPTS FOR WARRANTY ITEMS AND VALUABLES

A simple solution is to staple the receipt to the owner's manual or accompanying literature and keep until the warranty expires or you no longer own the item. If there is no manual or literature, mark the receipt SAVE and store with miscellaneous receipts.

Another solution is to store all receipts for valuables and warranty items in a large envelope with receipts filed in smaller envelopes by categories such as jewelry, furnishings, appliances, and electronics in a fire- and burglar-resistant safe or safe-deposit box, along with your home inventory list and photos.
(see also Manuals, Product; Receipts, Miscellaneous; Storage Solution, page 168)

RECEIPTS, MISCELLANEOUS

Collect ATM, cash, and credit card receipts in a small plastic envelope with divided sections. Save only until

(continued)

Never store anything in your oven. *You* might remember to remove it before lighting the oven, but someone else may set it on fire!

you verify amounts on your bank and credit card statements and then shred all except those receipts needed for tax purposes. If you decide to return an item or discover that the product is defective, however, you might wish you had the receipt.

A simple solution is to store selected receipts in a 13-pocket, accordion-style paper organizer with divider tabs for each month. Use the extra pocket to store receipts you want to keep beyond the year. Accordion files can be purchased in office supply stores in wallet or letter size and in a variety of colors and styles. Throughout the year, file receipts in the appropriate month. At the end of 12 months, empty the current month of last year's receipts (it's a good idea to shred them) and file the current month's receipts. That way, you'll always have a full year of receipts at your fingertips should you need them.

Keep in mind that you probably don't need to save receipts for groceries, drugstore sundries, and other items that you are not likely to return. And make sure the receipts you do save identify the item you purchased and the store (not all merchants personalize their receipts); if not, make a note on the receipt. Store the accordion file on a shelf or in a cabinet. A

(continued)

Communications center

A communications center assists the daily flow of information between family members. Establish a central spot (perhaps in the kitchen or family room) for mail, notes, permission slips, and other key papers. Use stackable trays, wall-mounted files, or standing accordion folders to create an inbox for each person. Put up a small bulletin board where you can pin up notices of upcoming activities and events.

Store items that are used often but frequently misplaced, such as keys and cell phones, on or near the notice board. A wall or desktop charging station is a handy place to store your electronic equipment, including chargers. Or look for a hanging wall organizer with special pockets for cell phones and iPods with a slit that allows you to connect to chargers plugged into the wall outlet behind it.

(see also Local Area Information; Notes; Storage Solution, page 160)

similar solution to the accordion file is to create a hanging file folder in a filing cabinet with the label MISCELLANEOUS RECEIPTS and the year, and either store them all in one interior folder or file by month. Or just put them all in a labeled box or tin and don't worry about sorting. After all, you're keeping them only in case you need them. When the container gets full, shred receipts you no longer need. You could also scan receipts into your computer.

RECIPES

Tag favorite recipes in cookbooks with sticky flags. Create your own cookbook from loose recipes that you have collected. Look to your cookbooks for organizational inspiration and then create tabbed dividers with categories such as BREAKFAST, EASY DINNERS, PASTA DISHES, DESSERTS, and whatever else suits you.

Sort all your loose recipes first by category or just start filing in a three-ring binder with the tabbed dividers in place. Slip full pages into three-hole-punched sheet protectors. You can also tape or glue recipe cards, clippings, and other smaller formats to a sheet of paper for easy insertion into the sheet protectors.

Look for dividers with pockets so you can file

(continued)

shoeboxes

- Use to organize photographs, recipes, stationery supplies, and memorabilia.
- Create a portable kit for bill paying — toss in unpaid bills as they arrive, along with calculator, checkbook, pen, envelopes, stamps — so that you can pick it up and carry it anywhere.
- Organize your dresser drawers to hold small pocketbooks, pantyhose, scarves, socks, and underwear.
- Have children sort small toys into shoeboxes — one for farm animals, one for monsters, one for doll clothes, and so on.
- Use them to hold craft supplies, string, ribbons, wrapping and decorating accessories.
- Keep CDs lined up tidily in a shoebox, or just store the jewel cases, if you have the CDs themselves somewhere else.
- Cover with contact paper or heavy gift-wrapping paper to liven them up.

OUT OF THE BOX
Organizer

Transforming Common Items into Storage Solutions

Recipes *(continued)*

untried recipes in each category. Or create a category for RECIPES TO TRY. For a very large collection, consider creating a book for each category. Label the binder covers and spines for easy reference.

(see also Storage Solution, page 168)

REMOTE CONTROLS

Give them a home: a basket or bowl on the coffee table, perhaps? A fabric pocket that hangs from an armchair is another solution; it can also hold your television listings. Or use double-sided tape and Velcro to attach it to the side of the television. Then train yourself to put them where they belong when not in use.

RIBBONS & BOWS, GIFT *(see Gift-Wrapping Paper and Accessories)*

RINGS

You can find a wide array of ring holders specifically designed for storing a small number of rings on your vanity. Or you could get creative and look around for an unusual container such as a soy sauce dish, miniature ramekin, tiny flowerpot, or an antique ashtray or teacup. Stacking jewelry tray organizers for rings are an inexpensive option for a larger collection.

SCHEDULES

Store event schedules, transportation schedules, and other frequently used schedules in a central location for easy access, such as on the refrigerator door. Magnetic clips and clipboards make it easy to store multiple schedules. You can also tape them to the inside of a cabinet or incorporate just the events you need into a family wall calendar or your personal calendar.

Another option is to put schedules into a family notebook or binder with other frequently referenced papers. If you need to refer to a schedule while away from home, make a reduced copy to carry in your purse or car or even your wallet.

(see also Storage Solutions, pages 168, 211)

SEEDS

Seeds should be stored in a cool, dry location away from sunlight and vermin. A common practice is to pour seeds into clearly marked envelopes and then seal and place one or more envelopes inside a ziplock bag and store it in an airtight container or freezer.

If you freeze seeds, bring them to room temperature before opening the package to prevent condensation, which can adversely affect germination.

(continued)

“

He is a wise man who does not grieve for the things which he has not, but rejoices for those which he has.

EPICTETUS

Seeds *(continued)*

You can also store seeds in airtight containers such as film canisters, prescription or medicine bottles, and canning jars; just be sure to label them. Reseal opened store-bought seed packets with tape and place them all in a ziplock bag. Most seeds will remain viable from one to five years.

SHEET MUSIC *(see Music Books and Sheet Music)*

SHEETS

Store fitted and flat sheets and matching pillowcases together as sets. Label linen closet shelves to identify bed size (KING, QUEEN, FULL, TWIN) or by room (MASTER, GUEST, CHILD 1, CHILD 2). If you store your linens in a dresser, designate a drawer for each type. If you have the space, store the sheets for each bed in the same room, perhaps in an extra drawer or on a closet shelf; an under-bed storage box is a good solution here.

(see also Linens)

SHOES

There are more ways to store shoes than you can shake a sock at. Store shoes off the floor with some type of shoe-organizing product; it makes it easier to clean

(continued)

vases

- A small, sturdy vase with a wide opening might be the perfect container for storing cooking utensils on the kitchen counter.
- Use one in a bathroom to hold hairbrushes and combs or toothbrushes and toothpaste.
- Use several attractive ones to serve silverware for a party or to keep a stash of chopsticks handy for takeout nights.
- Collect coins in a pretty vase rather than using a plain old jar.
- A small vase can hold pens and pencils on your desk.
- Use a tall one to hold all your knitting needles for quick and easy access. Brightly colored yarn balls in a glass vase are beautiful as well as practical.

Shoes *(continued)*

the floor and it looks a lot neater. Before you buy, count your shoes (and take the opportunity to weed out any pairs you haven't worn in a while).

You may want to sort a large collection by color or style: sandals, sporty, flats, low heels, high heels. Make it easy to retrieve and put away everyday shoes; others can be stored in a more out-of-the-way location like a high closet shelf. Shoe storage solutions:

» Freestanding shoe racks (shelf or carousel type)
» Shoe cabinets (come in different configurations)
» Hanging shoe organizers for the closet
» Pocket-style shoe organizers that hang on a door
» Shoe trolleys that roll under the bed
» Do-it-yourself or custom built-in shoe cubbies
» Clear plastic stackable shoeboxes

I prefer the last option — I buy them by the case and stack them on shelves. An alternative is to store shoes in their original boxes with a label or a photo of the shoes attached to the outside.

If you remove your shoes when entering your home, place a basket or shoe rack by the door to collect your shoes as well as those of your guests. *(see also Boots; Leather Items; Storage Solutions, pages 153, 224)*

S

ONE-MINUTE SOLUTION

A simple solution for storing shoes in a child's room and in entryways is to toss them all in a basket or plastic storage bin. You might have to dig around to find a matching pair, but it makes putting them away really easy.

SHORTS *(see Clothing: Shorts)*

SILVERWARE AND UTENSILS

Keep in a special tray designed to store silverware and utensils in a drawer. I prefer mesh-wire trays that lift out so I can easily clean the drawer surface underneath when needed.

Store real silver cutlery in an airtight container or ziplock bags to seal out air and prevent tarnishing.

S

SKIRTS *(see Clothing: Skirts)*

SLIDES *(see Negatives and Slides)*

SLIPPERS

If you don't have a designated storage place for your slippers, how will your dog be able to fetch them? I keep mine on the floor directly below my robe, which hangs on a hook in my bedroom closet.

You might also choose to store slippers under or near your bed or dresser, or near the entryway where you change out of your shoes or boots.

(see also Shoes)

SNOW TIRES

Hang on large hooks from garage rafters to keep floor space clear. Or stack them in a corner in the basement or crawl space. Putting them in large plastic trash bags keeps your clothes and hands clean when moving them.

SOCIAL SECURITY CARD

Do not carry your Social Security card in your wallet. Store in a fire- and-burglar resistant safe or bank safe-deposit box.

ONE-MINUTE SOLUTION

Rather than storing unmatched socks in a sock drawer, keep a small bin or basket for strays in the laundry room. If you're looking for a mate, you'll know where to find it.

SOCIAL SECURITY STATEMENT

Review for accuracy when it arrives and then file in a locked filing cabinet for safekeeping. Shred the old one when a new one arrives.

SOCKS/PANTY HOSE *(see Clothing: Socks and panty hose)*

S

Storage Solution

Shoe bag organizer

This has to be one of the most versatile organizers ever made — and it's inexpensive. A hanging shoe bag organizer with clear plastic pockets can be hung in a mudroom to store keys, outgoing mail, videos to return, mittens and gloves, hats, the dog's leash and waste bags, pet treats, and more.

Hang one on the back of a door to store cleaning supplies in the utility room or in the bathroom to store toiletries, hair care tools, magazines, and washcloths.

It's a great solution in the garage for storing small hand tools and other items such as work gloves, tape measures and pencils, or gardening tools and supplies.

Hung on the back of a door in a kid's room, it's handy for storing small toys, dolls, and stuffed animals. You may find one useful in the pantry or for sorting and storing craft items as well.

Hang one on a rod in a bedroom closet for storing underwear, socks, panty hose, and tights (no folding required!) or for storing rolled belts, scarves, or ties. And, oh yes — you can use it to store shoes too!

film canisters

These handy containers with their tightly fitted lids can hold a lot of little stuff:

- 20 quarters for the Laundromat
- Safety or straight pins (tape one to the lid or the side for quick visual label)
- A travel supply of vitamins and other supplements, or even a couple of dollops of lotion or shampoo
- Seeds for planting next season
- Salt and pepper for picnics and camping
- A serving of salad dressing for a brown-bag lunch
- Beads, buttons, and other small craft supplies
- Tacks, screws, paper clips

SPICES

You can organize your spices alphabetically if you'd like, but I prefer to organize by type such as baking spices, dried herbs, whole spices, and ground spices. Store with labels facing out in a spice rack or two-tiered turntables (my favorite). I also recommend spice organizers that screw into shelves and drop down for easy access as well as door-mounted spice rack and drawer organizers.

- » Do not store spices in cabinets over the stove or on either side of the oven, as the heat will decrease their shelf life.
- » Do not store in direct sunlight and keep away from moisture (use a dry measuring spoon and do not sprinkle directly into a steaming pot).
- » Use tightly capped containers.
- » Discard all extracts that are more than four years old, except pure vanilla, which lasts indefinitely.
- » If there is no "best by" date on the bottle, replace herbs and spices if the color has faded or if the aroma is weak when you rub or crush the spice or herb in your hand. Seasoning blends should be replaced within one or two years.

SPORTS EQUIPMENT AND GEAR

Gather all sports equipment in one place. Designate a sports zone in your garage, storage shed, or basement. There are many types of garage wall organizers available at a wide range of price points. If you don't have built-in shelves or cabinets, consider investing in a large freestanding storage unit with interior shelves and doors.

Organize shelves with labeled storage containers or plastic milk crates for keeping helmets and gloves, camping or hiking gear, sports shoes, field hockey sticks, balls, and other items that go with various activities.

Use wall mounts or install a ready-made pulley system from the ceiling of the garage to get bicycles and kayaks or canoes off the floor. Store boating supplies such as paddles and life vests inside the kayaks or canoes.

No garage or shed? Consider whether a large hall closet might be put to better use as a storage place for sports equipment and gear instead of coats. Remove the clothes rod and replace with deep, sturdy shelving. *(see also Storage Solutions, pages 27, 175)*

S

ONE-MINUTE SOLUTION

It's easy to toss clothes you intend to wear again over a chair or even on the floor. But it's almost as easy to hang them on a hook on the back of your bedroom or closet door. Look for over-the-door racks or hooks with removable adhesive backing if you prefer not to use screw-in hooks or if you have hollow doors.

STEMWARE

To help prevent chipping the rims, store upright with stems down. Alternatively, install a stemware rack under a wooden cabinet or shelf on which you can hang wine stems for compact storage. Adjust shelves to maximize storage space within the cabinet by making the distance between shelves just tall enough to slide glasses in and out.
(see also Glassware)

S

STOCK AND BOND CERTIFICATES

Store in a fire- and burglar-resistant safe until sold.

SUITCASES

The more often you travel, the more conveniently your suitcase(s) should be stored. Three handy places to store suitcases are:

- On a shelf in your clothes closet
- Under your bed
- In a hall or guest room closet

It's a smart idea to store travel accessories such as a travel-sized hair dryer, a neck pillow, and a packed toiletries case inside your most frequently used suitcase. Infrequently used suitcases can be stored in the attic, basement, or garage. Store them inside each other, if possible, to save space and up off the floor to get them out of the way.

(see also tips on page 44)

SUITS *(see Clothing: Suits)*

SUNGLASSES *(see Eyeglasses and Sunglasses)*

SWEATERS *(see Clothing: Sweaters)*

S

TABLE LEAVES

The more often you use the leaves, the more accessible they should be. You may be lucky enough to have just the right storage space in a nearby closet or pantry. Otherwise, look for hidden storage space under or behind a nearby sofa or dining room hutch or under a guest bed.

Wrap leaves in a couple of layers of packing paper or bubble wrap, or use an old sheet or blanket to help prevent scratches and discourage dust. You can also purchase specially designed storage bags for protecting table leaves.

TABLE LINENS

Store tablecloths, runners, and napkins in a hutch or buffet if you have one in the dining room, or in a kitchen drawer, on a kitchen cabinet shelf, or on a pantry shelf. A hallway closet might present a storage option, depending on the configuration of your house. Holiday linens can be boxed and stored in the attic or with seasonal decorations until they are needed.

Iron before putting away so they are ready for use when you need them or at most need a light touch-up. *(see also Linens)*

T

lunch boxes

- They make good portable toy storage for little ones on the go; also useful for storing small things like seed packets.
- Use one to hold your button collection or a small sewing kit.
- Find a fun or funky one to hold the television and other remotes, to store extra hand towels or toilet tissue in a powder room, and to keep makeup and other toiletries in.
- Use them to hold a separate supply of craft items for each child — no more fighting over who gets the purple crayon!
- Turn one into a first-aid kit.
- Store plastic ware, straws, food container lids, cookie cutters, and other items in the kitchen.

TAKE-OUT MENUS *(see Local Area Information)*

TASKS

If you don't want to lose that list of things to do, store it in the same place every time you make one. I list all of my tasks on my computer in Outlook where I can sort them by date due, priority, and category such as personal or work-related tasks. For certain tasks, such as "Pick up the dry cleaning," you might use an online reminder service that will give you a call at a specific time.

If you prefer a written list, keep a master list of things to do and select no more than three to ten items for your daily to-do list. Estimate how long each task will take so you can more effectively plan your day. Or assign 1-2-3 or A-B-C priorities to each task.

TAX RECORDS

The IRS advises the following: "You should keep your records in an orderly fashion and in a safe place. Keep them by year and type of income or expense. One method is to keep all records related to a particular item in a designated envelope" (IRS Publication 552: *Recordkeeping for Individuals*). Scanning paper to electronic images is also an acceptable means of storing tax records.

Create a holding place for receipts, statements, and other documentation that you will need at the end of the year to prepare your income tax return. One simple solution is to create and store a hanging file folder or accordion-style folder labeled TAXES and the year with one interior folder labeled INCOME and one EXPENSES. Or purchase a ready-made tax-filing system.

If you are not sure if you need to save a document for tax purposes, err on the safe side and save it in your current-year tax file. Previous-year tax returns and documentation can be stored in a filing cabinet drawer or in a labeled cardboard file box in a more out-of-the way place, such as the upper shelf of a closet.

Tax professionals recommend keeping all of your tax returns forever and keeping supporting documentation for up to six full tax years. Be aware that if you do not file a return or file a fraudulent return, you should hang on to your documentation indefinitely, as there is no time limit for the IRS to question those returns.

(see also Storage Solutions, pages 188, 196)

T

ONE-MINUTE SOLUTION

Enter the time and location of ticketed travel or events on your calendar, along with any other pertinent details, including confirmation numbers and where you put the tickets!

TICKETS

Put tickets where you are not likely to forget them. My husband and I put event tickets in the drawer where we keep our car keys. When we leave the house, we grab the keys and the tickets. You might clip them onto the pages of your calendar or put them in a basket near the calendar. Or you could put them in the glove box of your car or keep them in your purse or wallet to make sure you have them when you get where you're going.

(continued)

I wish I had a talent for dropping things as well as taking on new ones. It gets to be quite a clutter after a while.

JOSHUA LEDERBERG

Tickets *(continued)*

Store all paper airline, bus, train, and cruise tickets, e-tickets, and itineraries in a folder or envelope labeled TRAVEL. Store it in a suitcase or briefcase. If you travel frequently, set up a hanging folder with "grab-and-go" folders labeled by event or city or date. Another option is to store travel or event tickets in a tickler file.

(see also Storage Solution, page 80)

TIES *(see Belts and neckties)*

TITLES, VEHICLE

Store in a fire- and burglar-resistant safe or safe-deposit box until sold.

TOILET TISSUE, EXTRA ROLLS

The best place to store at least one extra roll is near enough to the toilet that you can reach it when you run out! If that means setting a reserve roll in all its glory on the tank top, so be it. But there are more attractive solutions available, including a wide variety of toilet roll holders and stands as well as lidded tanktop baskets.

(continued)

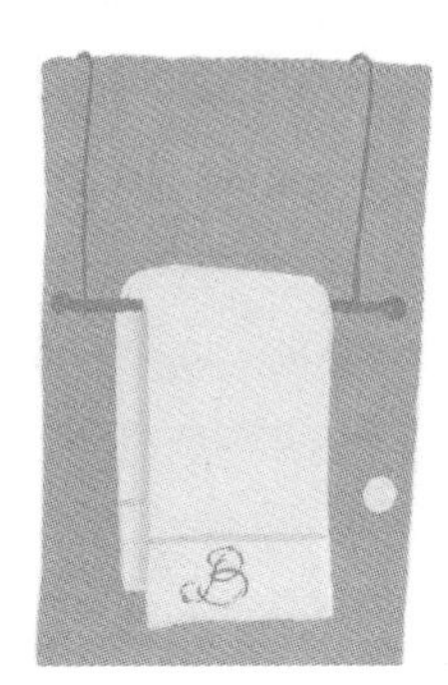

Bathroom storage

If you have lots of people in your house using towels, install additional rods, rings, or hooks to match or complement existing ones. If you have no available wall space, can't find your screwdriver, or aren't at all handy, there are some simple solutions that require no installation. Look for towel racks that hang over the shower door, back of the bathroom door, and front of cabinet doors.

Here's a brilliant idea: Replace your existing shower curtain rod with a dual rod that has an inner rod for the shower curtain and an outer rod for towels.

(see also Linens; Storage Solutions, pages 70, 140)

Toilet Tissue, Extra Rolls *(continued)*

If you buy toilet tissue in bulk, you've probably already got a place where you stash the rest of your supply, which might be in every cabinet in every bathroom, on a shelf in your clothes or linen closet, or in the laundry room or garage. Small-home and tiny-apartment dwellers can make use of under-bed space for storing toilet tissue as well as other paper goods and pantry items.

(see also Bulk Food and Paper Items)

TOILETRIES

Stand in front of your sink. Reach both arms out in front of you and then to the sides. Somewhere in that arc you just created is a good place to store toothpaste, deodorant, and other personal-care items you use every day. It might be a drawer, a shelf in the medicine cabinet, or a basket or bin hidden away under the sink.

Another solution where multiple family members share a bathroom is to give each person a wire basket that can be stored on a shelf.

It might be tempting to leave items out on the countertop — not that there's anything wrong with that! — but if you do, storing items on a decorative

tray or in a basket will result in a less cluttered look. Plus, the less you leave out, the easier it is to clean the countertop. Consider moving overstocks to a nearby closet, perhaps a bedroom or linen closet, or keeping under a bed in storage containers.
(see also Bath Supplies; Cosmetics; Storage Solutions, pages 60, 224)

TOOLS AND HARDWARE

Group tools and hardware into major categories such as automotive, electrical, plumbing, woodworking, general household, and painting. Then sort within categories: for example, screwdrivers, wrenches, chisels. Toss tools you no longer need or use into one or more boxes to give away or sell. If you can't bear to do that yet, at least pack them up and get them out of your immediate storage area.

Store the tools and supplies you use most often within easy reach. Store less frequently used items on upper shelves, under your workbench, or at the back of cabinets. Hanging is preferable to shelving items because it keeps tools more visible and accessible. Use pegboard and hooks to hang power tools and large hand tools, such as saws and hammers. Use a marker to trace the silhouette of each tool onto the pegboard for a visual reminder of where it goes.

Sort hardware by type — nuts, bolts, screws, nails, and fasteners — and sort within type by size. Store in a hardware drawer organizer or in glass jars with the lids screwed into the bottom of a shelf or cabinet. The underside of an open basement staircase might make a great place to mount the jars. Store other supplies in labeled plastic storage containers on shelves, grouped by category.

(see also Storage Solution, page 224)

TOWELS

If you don't have a linen closet or enough room to store towels with other linens, store towels in bathrooms, folded and stacked by size on shelves or rolled in a large basket. Alternatively, storing towels in the laundry room makes it easy to put them away straight from the dryer. Consider implementing a system of color-coded towels for family members.

Keep clean, dry beach and pool towels handy in the garage or mudroom in a laundry basket or large canvas or plastic tote bag. Another option is to provide a series of hooks (one per family member) or

T

If storage space is limited, consider rotating toys. Leave out some to play with now and put the rest into temporary storage. If the kids don't ask for them, you know that it's okay to donate them.

a freestanding towel rack for handy storage of pool towels. Towels can also be stored in a weatherproof container in the pool area for easy access.
(see also Linens)

TOYS

Toy boxes are one of the least ideal storage solutions. Why? Because kids have to take out all the toys to find the one they're looking for. A better solution is to place open storage bins or crates on shelves or tack crates on their sides to create cubbies. To make room for toy storage in a family or living room, consider partitioning off a toy storage space with a divider screen or repositioning a sofa to make room behind it.

Crazy as it might sound, your best solution could be to transform a hall closet or pantry into a toy storage area; hang coats on a coat rack in the front hall or in individual clothes closets or store pantry items in cabinets instead.

Whatever you do, make it easy for kids to put away their own toys. Sort toys into categories such as balls, dolls, cars, and animals. It helps to label bins using pictures for younger children to identify what goes where. Place bins or crates at a reachable height for children. Train children to put away a toy before grabbing a new one.

(see also Games/Puzzles)

TROPHIES AND AWARDS

If they're important to you, display trophies, plaques, and framed awards on a bookshelf or bookshelves large enough to hold your entire collection. Or install a display ledge around the perimeter of the room

(continued)

Not what we have, but what we enjoy, constitutes our abundance.

JOHN PETIT-SENN

(measure your tallest trophy to determine the correct distance from the ceiling).

Pin award ribbons in shadow boxes (available at art supply stores) that can be hung on a wall. Organize photos, news clippings, certificates, and other memorabilia in a scrapbook.

If you don't want to display the awards, don't have the space for them, or the awards belong to a child who no longer wants them, consider taking photographs of them and making 8-by-10-inch (20 by 25 cm) prints to include in a scrapbook. Or remove the plaque from the stand and put it in a scrapbook with other items or in a photo album next to a photo of the trophy being presented. Then discard the trophies.

TROUSERS *(see Clothing: Pants and jeans)*

ONE-MINUTE SOLUTION

What's in *your* wallet? Remove frequent flier and shopper cards and put back only those you use at least once a week. Store the rest in a business card case and toss it in your purse. For accounts where you are not required to show the actual card, type a list on a credit-card size slip of paper, laminate it and store in your wallet.

UMBRELLAS

Why is it that you never have one when you need it? Store several portable or folding umbrellas in places where they might come in handy: the door well of your car, outside pocket of your overnight bag or gym bag, and briefcase or purse. Also store an umbrella or two or three near the door you use most frequently.

UNDERWEAR *(see Clothing: Underwear)*

V

VACUUM CLEANER

If possible, store your vacuum cleaner close to the center of your home; e.g., in a hall closet or laundry room/mudroom cabinet. Store in a way that makes it easy to take out and put away. Store bags and other accessories on a nearby shelf or hang them in a tote bag from a hook.

VASES

Vases can be stored throughout the house as decorative items on bookshelves and tables or all together in one cabinet. One of the best cabinets for storing vases is the one over the refrigerator or microwave; it is too warm there to store perishable items, but perfect for items that do not require frequent access.
(see also tips on page 219)

VETERAN'S PAPERS

Store in a bank safe-deposit box.

VIDEOTAPES

As with CDs and DVDs, the simplest way to store videotapes is to shelve and organize them into categories, such as G-rated, horror, drama, comedy, and romance. Videotapes may also be arranged and stored spine up in lidded containers, or in a large drawer, if there is one near the entertainment center. Keep them away from direct sunlight and heat sources.
(see also CDs and DVDs)

VITAMINS

Store vitamins in a cool, dry, dark place in the original bottle or other airtight container and keep out of reach of children. The worst place to store vitamins is in a bathroom or kitchen; both are frequently hot or humid, and this will shorten the shelf life. It's okay to store a bulk supply of vitamins in the refrigerator provided you take them out and allow the container to warm up to room temperature before opening.

That which we elect to surround ourselves with becomes the museum of our soul and the archive of our experiences.

THOMAS JEFFERSON

W

WALLET ITEMS

Make a copy of everything you carry in your wallet or make a list of all the items with account numbers and customer service numbers. Store the list in a locked file cabinet at home.

When traveling, take a copy of the list and keep it in your suitcase in the event that your wallet is lost or stolen. You can also give a copy to a trusted friend or family member.

WARRANTIES, PRODUCT

Staple product receipts to warranty certificates or product manuals and keep for as long as you own the item.

(see also Manuals, Product)

WARRANTIES, VEHICLE

Store in a fire- and burglar-resistant safe or bank safe-deposit box until the vehicle is sold.

tissue boxes

Recycle empty tissue boxes to create attractive, functional containers that you can use in and around your home.

- Fill with plastic grocery bags to use for lining wastebaskets, for disposing of dirty diapers, or in your car for trash bags.
- Use as a mini-trash receptacle for disposing of lint and used dryer sheets.
- Store clothespins on a shelf in your laundry room.
- Stash microfiber dusting cloths in strategic places around your home for quick cleanups.
- Remove the top of a tall tissue box and about two-thirds of one side, which becomes the front. Place in your pantry or cupboard for "filing" gravy and spice packets.

“

Organized people are just too lazy to look for things.

BERTRAND RUSSELL

WILLS

Give the original to the executor or administrator of your estate. Store a copy in a safe-deposit box or fire- and burglar-resistant safe. Be aware that if you store the original in a bank safe-deposit box registered in your name only, the box will be sealed upon your death. Your executor or trustee will, at minimum, need to present a copy of your death certificate plus a copy of your will in order to obtain access to the original will. In some states, opening the box may require a court order, which could take weeks. You may want to name your executor as a joint owner of your safe-deposit box and give him or her a key to it.
(see also Legal-Sized Papers; Storage Solution, page 32)

WINE

For short-term storage (less than six months), store wine in racks at the lowest stable temperature possible in a dark location such as a closet or pantry, away from any items with strong odors. Do not store unopened wine in the refrigerator or near any source of light, heat, or vibration.

Store unopened bottles on their side and at 70 percent humidity or higher to keep the corks moist

W

and minimize evaporation. Refrigerated wine cabinets keep wine at the perfect temperature and humidity and they come in a variety of sizes and styles. More serious collectors and do-it-yourselfers can turn an ordinary room into a wine cellar with a prefabricated, insulated wine-room kit.

For optimum long-term storage of wine (six months or more), the most important rule is to keep temperature constant. The ideal temperature to store wines is 55 to 58°F, although 40 to 65°F (4 to 18°C) is acceptable. Lower temperatures will slow the aging process and higher temperatures will speed it up.

There's at least one free software program that allows you to keep track of your inventory and search by producer, vintage, varietal, price, and more. There's also a product that automatically inputs data about each bottle as you scan the bar code.

(see also Liquor)

WINEGLASSES *(see Stemware)*

WRAPPING PAPER *(see Gift-Wrapping Paper and Accessories)*

WREATHS, SEASONAL *(see Decorations, Seasonal)*

Reduce clutter and eliminate the time, effort, and space required to store paper by:

- Keeping track of your calendar, tasks, and contacts.
- Paying bills online.
- Scanning and store receipts and records on your computer.

plastic rain gutters

A creative alternative to shelving!

- Measure to fit and then hang white plastic gutters along a wall in a playroom or bedroom to display books, small dolls, beanbag toys, and other small playthings.
- Or hang several pieces in a closet, one above another, to store rolls of wrapping paper, bows, ribbons, tape, scissors, gift tags and other gift-wrapping accessories.
- Hang a short piece underneath a chalkboard to store an eraser and chalk or below a bulletin board to store extra pushpins, a small pad of paper, pens, and items too bulky to tack up.
- A length of gutter hung just above the surface of a workshop table can hold frequently used hand tools and other small items.

X Y Z

X

X-RAYS

Maybe you broke your arm 10 years ago, injured your knee skiing last winter, or needed braces to correct your bite. And you still have the X-ray, CT, or MRI scan to prove it! Perhaps it's a bit of memorabilia to you, in which case you might want to store it with other mementos. You also could store it with your medical records. But there are three things you should keep in mind:

» X-rays degrade quickly when exposed to high heat, humidity, or strong sunlight.

» The X-ray or scan you have is a copy of the original scan.

» Your original X-rays may still be on file with your health care facility.

Laws vary from state to state, but the American Medical Association and American Medical Records Association both recommend a minimum retention period of 10 years. Some facilities retain records even longer. At minimum, records for minors must be saved for at least seven years; many states extend

ONE-MINUTE SOLUTION

When discarding X-rays or other medical scans, cut off personally identifiable information such as your Social Security number and discard it separately.

this policy to when the patient is age 18 or 21. In any event, most X-rays are now stored in digital form. It's a good idea to ask for an electronic copy on disk that you can store with your medical records.

(see also Medical Records; Memorabilia)

YARN

Store your stash in lidded plastic containers to protect it from dust, moths, and other insect infestation as well as water damage. Organize by type such as sock yarn, wool, acrylic, or cotton or by weight. Label and store containers on shelves in a closet, workroom, or other climate-controlled area in your home.
(see also Storage Solution, page 153)

YEAR-END STATEMENTS

Once you receive year-end statements from banks, financial lenders, and other companies, you can discard monthly and quarterly statements. Store year-end statements with your tax documentation.
(see also Tax Records)

YOGA EQUIPMENT

Store your mat, blocks, straps, pillows, and other equipment in a closet or other space near the place where you indulge in your practice; e.g., in a large tote bag on the floor of your closet or under your bed for those early-morning sun salutations.

If you practice yoga outside your home, consider storing your equipment in the trunk of the car. Make

(continued)

Interestingly, according to modern astronomers, space is finite. This is a very comforting thought — particularly for people who can never remember where they have left things.

WOODY ALLEN

it easy to transport everything you need by keeping it all in a large mesh bag or other carrying bag.

ZINNIA SEEDS *(see Seeds)*

ZOO ACTIVITIES *(see Local Area Information; Schedules)*

Ziplock bags

Clear plastic resealable bags are one of my favorite storage tools. Use them to corral items you want to keep together in a drawer, such as cookie cutters, batteries, sewing items, and plastic utensils. Use labeled ziplock bags to keep extra parts, such as screws and bolts, from getting lost in the workshop or garage.

When traveling, pack small related items such as toiletries, medications, food and utensils, underwear, socks, and chargers in separate plastic bags. The clear bags protect your belongings and make it easy to find what you need.

When you unpack at home, just leave the bags in your suitcase to reuse on your next trip.

(see also Arts and Crafts Supplies; Buttons; Chargers and Cables)

INDEX

U

V

W

Z

Other Storey Titles You Will Enjoy

Dorm Room Feng Shui, by Katherine Olaksen.
An introduction to feng shui for the college student, with practical tips for clearing the chi in every dorm room.
144 pages. Paper. ISBN 978-1-58017-592-0.

The One-Minute Cleaner Plain & Simple, by Donna Smallin.
The perfect handbook for busy people — clean smarter, not harder!
288 pages. Paper. ISBN 978-1-58017-659-0.

The One-Minute Organizer Plain & Simple, by Donna Smallin.
Quick, painless fixes to offer solutions to the busy person's daily battle with clutter, both physical and mental, one minute at a time.
288 pages. Paper. ISBN 978-1-58017-584-5.

Organizing Plain & Simple, by Donna Smallin.
A gentle guide that helps readers gain control over everyday disorder and be better prepared for life's big events.
320 pages. Paper. ISBN 978-1-58017-448-0.

Unclutter Your Home, by Donna Smallin.
Hundreds of practical ideas for sorting, evaluating, and getting rid of all those unwanted items.
192 pages. Paper. ISBN 978-1-58017-108-3.

Wabi Sabi: The Art of Everyday Life, by Diane Durston.
A giftbook that celebrates nature's simplicity and imperfection.
384 pages. Paper. ISBN 978-1-58017-628-6.